SHEFFIELD HALLAM UNIVERSITY
LEARNING CENTRE
COLLEGIATE CRESCENT CAMPUS
SHEFFIELD S10 2BP

101 776 547 2

ND THE LAW

Unmarried heterosexual cohabitation is rapidly increasing in Britain and over a quarter of children are now born to unmarried cohabiting parents. This is not just an important change in the way we live in modern Britain; it is also a political and theoretical marker. Some commentators see cohabitation as evidence of selfish individualism and the breakdown of the family, while others see it as just a less institutionalised way in which people express commitment and build their families. Politically, 'stable' families are seen as crucial—but does stability simply mean marriage? At present the law in Britain retains important distinctions in the way it treats cohabiting and married families and this can have deleterious effects on the welfare of children and partners on cohabitation breakdown or death of a partner. Should the law be changed to reflect this changing social reality? Or should it—can it—be used to direct these changes?

Using findings from their recent Nuffield Foundation funded study, which combines nationally representative data with in-depth qualitative work, the authors examine public attitudes about cohabitation and marriage, provide an analysis of who cohabits and who marries, and investigate the extent and nature of the 'common law marriage myth' (the false belief that cohabitants have the same legal rights as married couples). They then explore why people cohabit rather than marry, what the nature of their commitment is to one another and chart public attitudes to legal change. In the light of this evidence, the book then evaluates different options for legal reform.

REFERENCE

Sheffield Hallam University
Learning and Information Services
Withdrawn From Stock

Cohabitation, Marriage and the Law

Social Change and Legal Reform in the 21st Century

ANNE BARLOW, SIMON DUNCAN, GRACE JAMES
and
ALISON PARK

·HART·
PUBLISHING

OXFORD AND PORTLAND, OREGON
2005

Published in North America (US and Canada) by
Hart Publishing
c/o International Specialized Book Services
5804 NE Hassalo Street
Portland, Oregon
97213-3644
USA

© Anne Barlow, Simon Duncan, Grace James and Alison Park, 2005

Anne Barlow, Simon Duncan, Grace James and Alison Park have asserted their right under the
Copyright, Designs and Patents Act 1988, to be identified as the authors of this work.

All rights reserved. No part of this publication may be reproduced, stored in a retrieval system,
or transmitted, in any form or by any mean, without the prior permission of Hart Publishing,
or as expressly permitted by law or under the terms agreed with the appropriate reprographic
rights organisation. Enquiries concerning reproduction which may not be covered by the
above should be addressed to Hart Publishing at the address below.

Hart Publishing, Salter's Boatyard, Folly Bridge,
Abingdon Road, Oxford OX1 4LB
Telephone: +44 (0)1865 245533 or Fax: +44 (0)1865 794882
e-mail: mail@hartpub.co.uk
WEBSITE: http://www.hartpub.co.uk

British Library Cataloguing in Publication Data
Data Available

ISBN 1 84113–433–3 (paperback)

Typeset by Compuscript, Shannon, Ireland
Printed and bound in Great Britain by
Page Bros, Norwich, England

SHEFFIELD HALLAM UNIVERSITY
LR
346.016
BA
COLLEGIATE CRESCENT

Contents

Acknowledgements

The research project that forms the backbone to this book was funded by the Nuffield Foundation, and we would particularly like to thank Sharon Witherspoon for her support of the project and its development. The members of the advisory group—Dame Margaret Booth, Carol Smart, Rebecca Bailey-Harris, Mark Harper and Mary Macleod—gave advice and feedback as the project progressed. Yunis Alam and Cilizia Armstrong-Gibbons carried out the supplementary ethnic minority group interviews, while Amanda Porter efficiently transcribed all the interviews. Thanks also to Richard Hart for being patient with writing delays. Last, but certainly not least, we would like to thank the many respondents who took part in our work and enabled this book to be written.

1

Introduction

1 SOCIAL QUESTIONS, LEGAL PROBLEMS, AND RESEARCH

There are three major contexts for this book. The first is the debate about the
nature of unmarried heterosexual cohabitation (hereafter 'cohabitation') and
the future of 'the family'. Numerically, cohabitation increased dramatically in
Britain, from 5 per cent to 15 per cent of all couples between 1986 and 1999
(Shaw and Haskey, 1999). More recent statistics suggest that 29 per cent of non-
married women aged under 60 were cohabiting in 2001/02, almost three times the
1986 rate. Furthermore, over a quarter of all children were born to cohabiting
families by the beginning of the twenty first century, and all these trends are predicted both to continue and to increase (National Statistics, 2004). Qualitatively,
as we review later, there is much evidence that cohabitation is often equated with
'do it yourself' marriage in people's minds, and it is no longer restricted to particular social groups or limited to short periods of people's lives. Cohabiting
couples can be just as committed as married couples and cohabitation is widely
accepted as suitable for both partnerships and bringing up children. Meanwhile,
marriage is in numerical decline and has been for some time. Between 1979 and
1995, the percentage of women in the British population who were married
decreased from 74 per cent to 56 per cent (Office for National Statistics, 2000).
By 2001 the marriage rate was at its lowest ebb since records began in 1897, with
fewer than 250,000 marriages per year in England and Wales, and only just over
half of these being first marriages.[1] This decline in the number of marriages has
been accompanied by a rapid rise in divorce of those who are married, with
around 40 per cent of all marriages at the turn of the century predicted to end in
divorce. Qualitatively, therefore, marriage has also changed; it self-evidently cannot be seen any longer as a commitment for life or as a necessary marker of
adulthood and respectability. The evidence (which we review later) also suggests

[1] The small rise in the marriage rate in 2000 (1.7 per cent) represents, it seems, romantic notions
of the significance of the millennium year itself rather than any real reversal in partnering behaviour
(Office for National Statistics, 2003).

a change in the content of marriage, with a more negotiated and conditional commitment between partners which is open to termination.

This increase in cohabitation and the decline in marriage have become political and theoretical markers. Some commentators see these trends as evidence of the rise of selfish individualism and the breakdown of the family (for example Dennis and Erdos, 1992; Fukuyama, 1999; Morgan, 2000). Others—probably in an equally extreme way—see cohabitation as the best partnering form for pursuing democratic and consensual 'pure relationships' in post-modern society, where we can no longer live under externally imposed codes even if we want to (for example Giddens, 1992; Beck-Gernsheim, 2000). Politically, 'stable' families are seen as crucial, especially by the current New Labour government in Britain which sees the revitalisation of social morality as vital for a sustainable economy and society (Barlow and Duncan, 2000). Unfortunately, however, this debate about the nature of family change has often been undertaken in a polemical or abstract manner, and both tendencies leave policy formulation without much purchase on the actual empirical nature of family change. Policy then comes to depend on simplistic assertions about the value of one family form (for example marriage) over another, combined with a focus on family failure rather than on what families actually do. There is therefore a need for empirical sociological research to provide some answers as to what these trends mean.

The second context is the problem with family law, at the beginning of the twenty-first century, as it affects cohabitants. While marriage and cohabitation, and the relation between them, have rapidly and possibly fundamentally changed, marriage alone—and often an outdated version of marriage—remains the keystone of family law. Cohabitation, in contrast, is often ignored in family law and, even when recognised, is treated only in a piecemeal and ad hoc way. Marriage gives partners substantial and automatic legal benefits which they do not possess as unmarried cohabitants. It is not that cohabitants do not have any legal rights, rather these rights are complex, confusing and nearly always inferior. They are hardly ever automatic. We will review the current legal situation for cohabitants in section 1.3 which follows, but the upshot is that those people—generally children and caring dependants—who are the most vulnerable in families, especially on breakdown or death, are particularly vulnerable as cohabiting family members because of this legal situation. Worse, because the law does give the impression that cohabitants are equal to married couples in some everyday situations—notably in the tax and benefit system—those directly affected are disarmed rather than forewarned. How this situation might be legally resolved is primarily a question for the law reform process.

The third context for this book is the link between these sociological and legal questions—should the law be changed and, if so, how can it be changed? This is quite a complex socio-legal question quite apart from the technicalities involved, because it immediately brings into focus a wider moral and political question about what the law is for and what it should do. Put simply, should law reflect social norms and behaviour, and so attempt to 'move with the times', or should it attempt to impose moral and social principles, and so try to direct behaviour? Can or should the law be used to encourage people to marry and reassert marriage as a social imperative? Or should we accept the change in social norms and behaviour and extend the family law protection and privilege previously reserved for married couples to cohabitants, who now also undertake traditional partnering and parenting roles? On what basis should such policy issues be decided and what other regulatory options might be pursued? Furthermore, following our answer to these questions the law could be changed, for different reasons, to different degrees and with different effects. Again, this is an issue to be elucidated by empirical socio-legal research.

In order to follow up these questions we undertook a major empirical study 'Family restructuring, the common law marriage myth and the need for legal realism' funded by the Nuffield Foundation from 2000 to 2002. This book is based on the results of the project. An overall aim was to strengthen the evidence base for the sociological, legal and socio-legal questions reviewed above, which remained weak despite some excellent pioneering studies (notably Jane Lewis' *The End of Marriage?* published in 2001). In order to accomplish this our more specific aims were to:

— Examine public attitudes about sexual relations, parenting, cohabitation and marriage;
— Explore the nature and impact of the 'common law marriage myth' whereby people falsely believe that cohabitants have the same legal rights as married couples;
— Provide an analysis of who cohabits, who marries and why;
— Investigate legal attitudes and beliefs about cohabitation and 'common law marriage', and about attitudes to legal reform;
— Assess options for legal reform in the light of the research findings.

In carrying out this research we were mindful of the criticism made by some (Deech, 1990; cf Eekelaar and Maclean, 1990; O'Donovan, 1993) that family law reform has been over-reliant on small-scale empirical studies which predicate proposals for reform on what prove to be inaccurately predicted social responses. In order to avoid this, our study used a combination of extensive research based on a nationally representative survey and in-depth intensive research based on a broad range of qualitative interviews. This combination, we claim, gives the research reported here a particularly robust empirical base. We will now review our research design in the next section (and see the Appendices for details).

2   APPROACHES AND METHODS—MIXING QUANTITATIVE AND QUALITATIVE DATA

For the research that underpins this book we adopted a 'mixed' design employing both extensive and intensive research, and using both quantitative and qualitative data. Extensive research aims to describe overall patterns and distinguishing features, for example the characteristics of a population of cohabitants. Usually (though not necessarily) this research uses quantitative data from large scale surveys including official statistics. While suitable for producing representative description, this design is weaker on explaining how and why these patterns have occurred. Intensive research in contrast seeks to answer the 'how' and 'why' questions by establishing what social agents like cohabitants actually do, believe or understand in the particular situations in which they find themselves. While it may be possible to roughly infer this from extensive research, intensive research can go further in identifying such social processes more directly and precisely. Intensive research usually (although again not necessarily) employs in-depth case study and qualitative methods. While therefore more powerful than extensive research in explanatory terms, intensive research is weak in providing representative descriptive information, although again this may be roughly inferred. In this way each research design has different strengths and weaknesses, and they should be seen as complimentary—although unfortunately they are often regarded as being in opposition to one another with strong tendencies to privilege one design over another (see Andrew Sayer 1992 for discussion on this point).

Mixing the two approaches enabled us to employ each research design, and use particular sorts of data, where most appropriate and so maximise the strength of each while compensating for their respective weaknesses. The extensive research was based on the British Social Attitudes (BSA) Survey undertaken in summer 2000 using information from 'standard' questions in the survey about social characteristics (like age, class, gender and occupation), as well as questions specific to this research. See Appendix 1 for details. Because of differences in the legal situation in Scotland, the research reported here used information from the 3,101 respondents living in England and Wales, but Anne Barlow has provided a detailed discussion about cohabitation in Scotland using the Scottish part of the survey (Barlow, 2002). This gave us nationally representative information about overall attitudes towards cohabitation and marriage, the social characteristics of the cohabitant population in Britain, the prevalence of the 'common law marriage myth', and cohabitants' preferences for legal reform.

The intensive research was based on 48 in-depth interviews with respondents who took part in the BSA survey. These were semi-structured, conversational interviews, and were conducted between April and September 2001. They were designed to elicit information on cohabitants' practices, beliefs and understandings in order to give us more detailed and contextualised information on why, and how, different sorts of cohabitant acted in particular ways. The interviews focused on three broad areas, as follows:

1 Practices of, experiences and attitudes to cohabitation/marriage.
2 Belief in common law marriage.
3 Views about legal reform.

Because the intensive research did not aim to produce representative description (the function of the extensive research) there was no need to attempt to set up a statistically representative sample of interviewees. Nor did this sample need to be large. Rather, small quotas of different sorts of cohabitant were taken, based on expectations of different behaviour as suggested by previous research findings. A particular advantage of basing our interview sample on the BSA survey respondent list was that we could find a range of cohabitant types, in contrast to most previous studies which have, by necessity, had to focus on particular and sometimes rather particularistic groups of cohabitant. We interviewed cohabitants and former cohabitants of different partnership and parental status, with different lengths of cohabitation, and covering a range of social divisions by gender, age, housing tenure, occupation and class. Basing the qualitative sample on the BSA survey also gave us the advantage of access to the standard survey information already gathered. However, all these 48 interviewees were White; the BSA survey, as a nationally representative sample, included few respondents from Black ethnic minority groups—none of whom we were successful in contacting. Small distinctive groups often make particular trends, practices and understandings highly visible. Because of this, they might also be particularly affected by legislative change. These issues are particularly pertinent in the case of some ethnic minority groups in Britain where we know from census evidence that British Africans/African-Caribbeans have particularly high rates of cohabitation, especially for parents with children (about double the national rate), while British Asians have especially low rates (less than 1 per cent). We therefore took small additional interview samples, outside the BSA sample frame, of eight British African/African-Caribbean current and former cohabitants living in Lambeth and Southwark in Inner London, and 17 British Asians living in Bradford, in West Yorkshire. Both areas hold high populations of these respective ethnic groups, and might therefore be expected to better maintain any particular cultural or social behaviours. See Appendix 1 for details of the interview sampling and Appendix 2 for the interview schedule.

3 THE PROBLEMS WITH COHABITATION LAW

The origins of our research, and of this book, can be traced back to the problems of cohabitation law in Britain. When practising as a family solicitor in Inner

London, one of the authors was increasingly troubled by the legal complexities and difficulties faced by cohabitants, for instance on separation, and the penalties many—and their children—were consequently subject to. Worse, many cohabitants thought they were protected by 'common law marriage', and so strong was this belief on occasion that some even walked out on hearing the true legal situation, searching for a 'real lawyer' who knew what they were talking about! This led to research on the characteristics of family law as it affected cohabitants (Barlow, 2001) and, subsequently, to the question of whether the law ought to be, and could be, changed to better this situation. Hence this research. We will begin, therefore, with a brief review of the problems with cohabitation law.

Formal marriage has always been the epicentre of family law, and particularly so since Lord Hardwicke's 1753 Marriage Act which withdrew legal recognition from informal 'common-law marriage'. Nonetheless, lawmakers could not totally ignore cohabitation, if only because of its popularity at certain times and places (see chapter 3 for discussion). In particular, in the 1970s and early 1980s a more inclusive or neutral approach to regulating 'marriage-like' cohabitants emerged, although this was reversed in the 1990s by the 'return to family values' ushered in by the then Conservative government. The succeeding Labour Government's agenda after 1997 of 'strengthening marriage' (see the Green Paper *Supporting Families*, Home Office 1998; Barlow and Duncan, 2000) consolidated this reversal, despite calls to include cohabitants in the legal process in a more cohesive way (for example the Law Society, 2002 and the Solicitors' Family Law Association, 2003). The only concession to cohabitants in the 1998 government blueprint was that 'perhaps information leaflets should be provided in Citizens Advice Bureaux' to better inform them of their legal disadvantage as compared with married couples, and this was followed in 2004 by a publicity campaign aimed at disabusing people from notions of common law marriage. Whether the new-style civil registrations for same-sex couples—but not for heterosexual couples, who it is claimed can choose marriage if they wish (DTI Women and Equality Unit, 2003a)—represents further strengthening of marriage or the thin end of the wedge in recognising cohabitation remains a moot point (see chapter 6).

The upshot of this lop-sided development is that the law accepts that married families should be regulated in a special and privileged way but is unclear about the status of cohabitation. Lawmakers have consequently responded to cohabitation in an ad hoc way on an issue by issue basis and sometimes the law treats cohabitants as married, sometimes ignores the relationship altogether and treats them as individuals, and in other instances treats them as a couple, but a couple which is inferior to their married counterparts. This is particularly problematic in relation to property and financial provision rights and remedies and overall cohabitation law is acknowledged to be complex, confusing and often illogical. At the time of our research the Law Commission was looking into the rights of homesharers including cohabitants, a task it had been assigned in 1992. The ten year delay in producing its Discussion Paper (not even a Report!) is symbolic of both the complexity of the legal issues and the salience of the political markers involved (Law Commission, 2002).

Perhaps the most obvious problem with this area of law is that whilst heterosexual cohabitation may in certain situations confer legal rights, there is no universal definition of such relationships. Broadly speaking inclusion in family law regulation has been reserved almost exclusively (at least until very recently) for the most marriage-like relationships, where a man and woman are living together 'as husband and wife' usually within a shared household, often for a minimum prescribed period of time and where there is or has been sexual intimacy. However, whether or not you are considered a cohabitant will depend on the statutory or judicial definition of cohabitation adopted in the context in which you are seeking to rely on such a status.

Some examples will demonstrate this point. In the social security field, s137 Social Security Contributions and Benefits Act 1992 provides that an unmarried couple is a man and a woman who are not married to each other 'but are living together as husband and wife otherwise than in prescribed circumstances'. *Crake v SBC* [1982] 1 All ER 498 set out a checklist of indicators of cohabitation which have been used by the courts in other contexts (see eg *Kimber v Kimber* [2000] 1 FLR 383). The indicators include two people of opposite sex; membership of the same household; stability and some duration of the relationship; financial support; sexual relationship; children of the relationship; and public acknowledgement of the relationship. Section 1(3) Fatal Accidents Act 1976 and s1A Inheritance Act 1975 are less extensive, and both simply require an eligible cohabitant applicant to have been living in the same household as the deceased, immediately before the death and for at least two years prior to this as the husband or wife of the deceased. This quasi-conjugal requirement in the Inheritance Act context was liberally interpreted in *Re Watson (Deceased)* [1999] 1 FLR 878. Here the issue of whether or not a couple were living as husband and wife should be addressed according to whether they would be considered so to be 'in the opinion of a reasonable person with normal perceptions' and stressed the multifarious nature of married relationships which for a couple in their late 50s need not include a shared bedroom or sexual relationship where a shared life which included 'wifely domestic tasks' (sic: cooking, cleaning, companionship) had been performed. However, for domestic violence order purposes, s62 Family Law Act 1996 includes as eligible 'associated persons', 'a man and a woman who, although not married to each other, are living together as husband and wife' which nonetheless should not be strictly interpreted in 'borderline cases' (*G v F* [2000] FCR 638). The Criminal Injuries Compensation Scheme was extended to opposite sex cohabitants in 1995 (and revised in 2001 to enable claims to be made by same-sex cohabitants). Paragraph 38a now extends the category of qualifying claimants to:

the partner of the deceased being only for these purposes,
(i) a person who was living with the deceased as husband and wife or as a same-sex partner in the same household immediately before the date of the death and who, unless formally married to him, had been so living for the two years before that date.

Most recently the Adoption and Children Act 2002—after much debate—is to allow unmarried couples to adopt. This Act stresses more the nature of the partnership and s144(b) defines a couple as 'two people (whether of different sexes or the same sex) living as partners in an enduring family relationship'.

The law in England and Wales does not, therefore, have any consistent definition of what constitutes cohabitation for legal purposes. How, then, does this inconsistency translate into practice in specific areas of law at different points in a relationship and how satisfactory is this situation?

During the Relationship

Whereas spouses on marriage automatically acquire occupation rights in the family home owned by their spouse (s30 Family Law Act 1996 (FLA 1996)), no such occupation rights are extended to cohabitants of either a rented or owner-occupied home. An occupation order granting occupation rights to a 'non-entitled' cohabitant who is not an owner or tenant of the family home can be made for a maximum total of 12 months, but this is an order likely to be sought where the relationship is breaking down, perhaps due to domestic violence (s36 FLA 1996). Unlike a married father, currently a cohabiting father does not automatically acquire parental responsibility (defined by s3(1) Children Act 1989 (CA 1989) as 'all the rights, duties, powers, responsibilities and authority which by law a parent of a child has in relation to the child and his property') for his child on birth, and thus cannot take formal decisions relating to his children, such as consenting to medical procedures or adoption (s2(2)(b) CA 1989). Although it can be acquired with the mother's consent by means of a simple procedure in which a parental responsibility agreement (in prescribed form) is signed and witnessed (s4 CA 1989), only five per cent of our BSA national survey of cohabitant fathers in England and Wales had done so, leaving the vast majority with legal duties and obligations but without any positive legal status in respect of their child. Whilst s111 Adoption and Children Act 2002 now gives parental responsibility to unmarried fathers who, with the mother, jointly register the birth of their child born on or after 1 December 2003, this is neither retrospective nor automatic on birth.

Although cohabitants, in contrast to spouses, have no legal duty to maintain each other during the relationship, on the application for any means-tested benefit or tax credit for the benefit of children, a cohabiting couple will be regarded as if they were married. Thus their means are aggregated to assess eligibility. However, unlike in the spousal context (see eg s27 Matrimonial Causes Act 1973

(MCA 1973)), if the partner in receipt of the benefit or tax credit fails to share this income with their partner, there is no legal redress. Neither do cohabitants benefit from capital tax concessions made to spouses. Thus whereas transfers between spouses are not subject to capital gains tax or inheritance tax (see Taxation of Capital Gains Act 1992 and Inheritance Tax Act 1984 respectively), cohabitants are treated as strangers liable to pay tax at the full rate.

On Relationship Breakdown

On relationship breakdown, there is certainly no 'divorce-law equivalent' for cohabiting couples. There is no duty to pay maintenance to a former cohabitant, nor to redistribute property between the partners according to family law principles when cohabiting partners separate. Instead, strict property law normally applies. This is the case even where one partner was totally financially dependent on the other during a long-term relationship and/or the other partner has gained advantage from the domestic and/or child care services provided. Where one or both cohabiting partners are (or claim to be) beneficial owners of the family home but no formal declaration of those interests has been made, on relationship breakdown, a declaration as to their respective beneficial interests in and an order for sale of the home can be made by the court (s14 Trusts of Land and Appointment of Trustees Act 1996). However, unless an order is made against this asset for the benefit of a minor child of the relationship—under provisions themselves likely to be less generous than those available to married parents (Schedule 1 CA 1989 discussed below), the proceeds will be divided in accordance with strict property law.[2] Perhaps most harshly, this is also the case where the cohabitants' relationship ends when their children have reached adulthood, leaving the primary caring partner, often female and of an age where it is more difficult to find employment or acquire new skills, without any legal remedy. This is well illustrated by the classic case of *Burns v Burns* [1984] Ch 317, a decision which is still good law (although some amelioration has been made where a non-owner has contributed to the purchase price—see *Midland Bank v Cooke* [1995] 2 FLR 915 and very recently *Oxley v Hiscock* [2004] EWCA Civ 546). After 19 years of unmarried cohabitation during which she raised two children, worked part-time and paid some of the household bills, Valerie Burns was unable to establish either an express or inferred 'common intention' sufficient to found a constructive trust under which she and her partner shared ownership of their family home. She thus had no beneficial interest in the home purchased in her partner's name and had no other legal redress available to her. She therefore left the relationship with

[2] See ss14 and 15 Trusts of Land and Appointment of Trustees Act 1996. Unless a resulting or constructive trust can be proved to have arisen, a non-legal owner will have no beneficial interest in the home. Even where such an interest has arisen, it may be impossible to avoid the home being sold, although s15 does require the court to have regard to the purpose for which the property was held under trust and the welfare of any minor occupying or reasonably expected to occupy the property as their home.

nothing. As was recognised by the Court of Appeal in that case, this is in sharp contrast to spouses, where family assets may be redistributed on divorce whether or not there are minor children, and largely regardless of the original ownership of assets.[3] Indeed, if anything recent developments in the case law governing financial provision on divorce have served to widen the gulf between married and cohabiting couples on relationship breakdown. On divorce, the division of assets between spouses must now be measured against a 'yardstick of equality' where assets exceed needs and provided there is no 'stellar' contribution by one party to the marriage, an equal division of the assets should be made (see *White v White* [2001] 1 AC 596; *Cowan v Cowan* [2001] 2 FLR 192; *Lambert v Lambert* [2002] 3 FCR 673). Where there is no such surplus of assets, the housing needs of the parties and especially those of the parent caring for any minor children (whose welfare must in all cases be the court's first consideration when deciding financial provision on divorce)[4] should be met first (*Cordle v Cordle* [2002] 1 WLR 1441). Thus a divorcing home-maker spouse where the major assets including the home are in the name of the other spouse will usually receive at least half of the assets, whereas an equivalent home-maker cohabitant in a similar position must prove an interest under a constructive trust to retain any share of the home, which, as Valerie Burns found to her cost, is often a difficult and always an unpredictable prospect for the economically weaker cohabitant partner (see further Barlow and James, 2004).

Some remedies (usually inferior to those for married couples) are now available to heterosexual cohabitants in respect of the rented family home. Schedule 7 FLA 1996 does now allow a non-tenant cohabitant to apply for a transfer of tenancy order on relationship breakdown. However, the criteria applied are less child-centric than in the married context in that again the welfare of the child is not the court's first consideration. Other factors, such as who was the original tenant and perhaps even the loss of any right to buy discount may weigh more heavily into the equation than in the divorce context. In the case of applications by non-tenant cohabitants, extra criteria must be applied including the nature of the relationship and currently the lack of the commitment given in marriage, although the presence of children 'for whom both parties have parental responsibility' and the length of time the parties have cohabited must also be taken into account (Schedule 7 para 5 and s41 FLA 1996). Technical difficulties also surround this remedy. To be eligible to apply for a tenancy transfer, the tenancy must

---

[3] See s25 MCA 1973 for the full list of criteria applied. This includes the standard of living during the marriage, the age of the parties and duration of the marriage, the parties' respective current and future income and assets, needs and resources as well as financial and (critically) non-financial contributions made and likely to be made to the welfare of the family by each of the parties and conduct it would be inequitable to ignore.

[4] S25(1) MCA 1973 states 'It shall be the duty of the court on deciding whether to exercise its powers under ss23, 24, or 24A above and if so, in what manner, to have regard to all the circumstances of the case, first consideration being given to the welfare while a minor to any child of the family who has not attained the age of 18 years.'

still exist at the date of the application, which may not be the case where the tenant partner has abandoned the tenancy or given notice to quit.

Whereas the child support legislation applies equally to separated married and unmarried parents, capital orders made routinely between divorcing spouses to share out the family assets are rarely made in the unmarried context, where the remedies that are available draw no distinction between former cohabiting parents and parents whose child was born of a more casual relationship. In principle lump sums, settlements and transfer of property orders between unmarried parents for the benefit of any child of the relationship are available (Schedule 1 para 2 CA 1989). However, because a cohabitant parent has no claim for financial provision against their former partner in their own right, orders made for the benefit of the children of cohabitant parents are far less generous than the combined package awarded to the resident parent and children on divorce. In *T v S (Financial Provision for Children)* [1994] 2 FLR 883 a so-called 'Mesher' order (delaying sale of the home until the youngest child finishes their education) was made whereby the father was ordered to purchase a home for the benefit of the five children of his cohabiting relationship, to be held on trust until the youngest child reached the age of 21. However, an order made at first instance that the home then be sold and the proceeds of sale divided between the children was overturned on appeal on the grounds that following decisions in the divorce context (eg *Chamberlain v Chamberlain* [1974] 1 All ER 33 followed in the unmarried context in *Kiely v Kiely* [1988] 1 FLR 248), it was inappropriate for the children to benefit as adults and furthermore, such an order would provide the former cohabitant mother with an inappropriate 'indirect windfall'. Instead, the whole of the home was ordered to revert to the father. Rather than expanding the remit of orders that can be made for the benefit of a child to compensate for the lack of adult claims, the provisions have largely been restrictively interpreted by the courts (see also *A v A (A Minor) (Financial Provision)* [1994] 1 FLR 657, *J v C (Child: Financial Provision)* [1999] 1 FLR 152; cf *F v G (Child: Financial Provision)* [2004] EWHC 1848). Thus in contrast to an equivalent home-maker spouse, the best that can be achieved for an economically dependent cohabitant who becomes the child's resident parent is a Mesher-style order, allowing the parent caring for the child to remain in the home until the youngest child reaches 21, with the property then being divided in accordance with strict property law entitlement.

On the Death of a Cohabitant

The law applicable in the event of the death of a cohabitant is also confused and contradictory. In the context of tenancy succession certain styles of rented family home, including Rent Act protected and assured tenancies, will automatically be transferred to a cohabitant on the death of the tenant partner regardless of how long the couple have cohabited, effectively treating the couple as if they were married from the outset (Schedule 1 para 2 Rent Act 1977). The cohabitant of a secure tenant, on the other hand, will only qualify if they have lived with the deceased tenant for at least 12 months prior to the death (s87 Housing Act 1985). Only a spouse will automatically inherit all or some of their spouse's estate where their husband or wife dies without making a will (s46 Administration of Estates Act 1925), although both a spouse and a cohabitant of at least two years' standing do now have the right to make a claim for financial provision under a deceased partner's estate where no or inadequate provision has been made for them by will (s1(1)(a) and (bA) Inheritance Act 1975). However, in the case of a cohabitant (unlike that of a spouse), the claim will be limited to such financial provision 'as it would be reasonable in all the circumstances for the applicant to receive for his (sic) *maintenance'*, (s2 Inheritance Act 1975, (emphasis added)). A spouse, in contrast, can expect to receive a more generous award, which is not limited to 'maintenance' and would normally be comparable to an award which would have been made on divorce. This 'similar but inferior' approach has also been taken with regard to claims under the Fatal Accidents Act 1976 which are open to a cohabitant whose partner of at least two years is killed by the negligence of a third party. Unlike a spouse, though, they are unable to recover the not insignificant statutory bereavement damages.

In yet other situations on death of a partner, cohabitants will be treated as strangers. Thus a cohabitant is not entitled to register the death of their partner, there is no exemption or reduction in inheritance tax payable on a gift left by a deceased cohabitant to their partner, pension payments to one partner will not be increased to maintain a dependant cohabitant nor will they have any pension or automatic entitlement out of their partner's estate on death. It is also interesting to note that whereas same-sex cohabitants, who until very recently were almost completely ignored by the law, could draw a small amount of comfort from the fact that they at least had the advantage of knowing where they stood, they too are now being drawn in to a process of ad hoc reform. This is aided by the wording of Schedule 1 to the Rent Act 1977 and the Human Rights Act 1998 (see *Fitzpatrick v Sterling Housing Association* [1999] 4 All ER 705 (HL) and most recently *Ghaidan v Godin- Mendoza* [2004] UKHL 30 in which the House of Lords have respectively extended tenancy succession of the Rent Act protected family home to same-sex couples first as members of their deceased partner's family and then as spouses).

It was these problems with cohabitation law that gave a first impetus to the research reported in this book. On the face of it, this confusing and complex legal situation, which incidentally also left large numbers of people—including children—in a vulnerable situation, cried out for reform. But would reform equate cohabitation and marriage, and was this desirable; furthermore, would cohabitants welcome such a reform, or did they prefer unregulated anonymity despite the vulnerability of weaker family members? In other words, should and ought the law to be changed? To answer this question, we needed up to date information on the prevalence, nature and perceptions of cohabitation, and public feelings about legal reform. It was only in the light of this information that any evaluation of the various possible models for law reform (or indeed the option of doing nothing) could sensibly be discussed. Hence our research agenda and the structure of this book, as outlined in the next section.

4 THE STRUCTURE OF THE BOOK

Chapter 2 describes the prevalence of unmarried heterosexual cohabitation in Britain, and the characteristics of cohabitants themselves, outlining the sort of people who cohabit and how they compare with married people. We then consider how attitudes to marriage and cohabitation have changed over time, highlighting how views about these two forms of relationship vary from one group to another. Overall we find that people's views of cohabitation and marriage have indeed changed over time. Whilst there is diversity of opinion, marriage has lost much of its social significance and cohabitation is increasingly practised and accepted. It is now more common for people to accept cohabitation as an alternative and a prelude to marriage, as traditional functions of the family (such as sexual intimacy, parenting and companionship) are no longer viewed as the exclusive domain of married couples.

Chapter 3 turns to the 'common law marriage myth'. Legal recognition of informal marriage was withdrawn in Britain in 1753 but, despite this, the notion of a legally recognised status of 'common law marriage' survives to the present day. The chapter shows that there is a widely held belief that heterosexual couples living together 'as man and wife' acquire 'marriage-like' rights and responsibilities through 'common law marriage', at least after a given period of time. The chapter describes the social extent of this 'myth', and goes on to examine how it operates in specific circumstances. We find that people make moral and social judgements about what seems right in balancing individual rights and family responsibilities, and assume—incorrectly—that the law mirrors what they see as sensible and just. Finally, we ask where people acquire their information about common law marriage and consider why this belief survives. In one sense the description 'myth' is appropriate to the widespread belief in the legal existence of common law marriage, in that this belief is factually incorrect—or at least greatly exaggerated—and is maintained through informal networks that use oral traditions rather than a written code. But in other ways this appellation 'myth' is inappropriate. This is because beliefs in common law marriage, while they do not reflect the formal law, do much more closely reflect how people experience—and regulate—their everyday lives. So rather than belief in common law marriage being simply myth as fantasy, it has a real basis in material, social life. This is what we call 'lived law'.

Chapter 4 goes on to ask why so many people cohabit—for at first sight, given the legal disadvantages of doing do—this seems like mass irrationality. The chapter examines three possible answers to this question. One is legal ignorance, or at least misinformation and lack of knowledge as articulated through belief in 'common-law marriage'. Another explanation is that cohabitants are less committed than married spouses, and so willingly avoid marriage. Finally, cohabitants may act according to different rationalities than the instrumental legal rationality lawmakers and government assume. The chapter shows that misinformation cannot explain the dramatic rise in cohabitation, if only because those who do not believe in common law marriage behave in almost exactly the same way. Nor are cohabitants less committed than married spouses, when we compare demographically and socially similar couples. Some sort of dramatic spread in lack of commitment, therefore, cannot explain the increasing levels of cohabitation in Britain. Rather, we find that large numbers of people in Britain perceive and experience cohabitation as a type of marriage. First, the majority now experience cohabitation as a prelude to marriage. However, 'marriage' in this case does not necessarily mean formal, legally registered marriage, for increasingly longer-term cohabitation is seen as a variety of marriage—such cohabitants are 'as good as married'. Even many of the minority who are opposed to marriage, either for reasons of principle or because of practical disillusionment, are in effect practising a variety of a marriage. Cohabitation is experienced as an adequate way of conducting committed relationships with other adults, and of bringing up children. Cohabitants are not acting irrationally, therefore, although many are left in a less secure legal position than married spouses. Lawmakers may therefore end up making a 'rationality mistake' where policy measures assume a type of decision making which does not match how people actually make decisions about their family lives.

Chapter 5 uses the information provided by chapters 2–4 to return to the legal issues. The focus of this chapter is a consideration of the tension between prevailing social attitudes to cohabitation and marriage law. This is exacerbated by the ambivalent response of legal policy makers to the unmarried cohabiting family. For the social phenomenon of family structuring away from marriage challenges the legitimacy of marriage-centred family law regulation which still, at the turn of the century, prevails in Britain. In particular, the chapter examines the significance of the divergence between social and legal norms.

Chapter 6 goes on to establish why our current marriage-centred family law, at the turn of the twenty-first century, should respond to the changed social reality described in the earlier chapters. We then go on to distil principles appropriate to guiding any legal reform. Finally, the chapter evaluates possible models for reform in the context of our findings, assesses current proposals for reform and examines the experiences of other jurisdictions facing the same challenges.

2

Marriage and Cohabitation in Britain: Changing Attitudes and Behaviour

1 INTRODUCTION

As the previous chapter demonstrates, official policy sees marriage as the best family form, especially when it comes to bringing up children. Unmarried cohabitation is virtually ignored (see, for example, the government's Green Paper *Supporting Families,* 1998). If marriage were the only real choice available, with cohabitation being rare, short-lived, or confined to particular groups, then relegating cohabitation to the footnotes of social and legal policy in this way might make little difference. However, current policy appears less easy to justify if marriage is no longer viewed as the only choice available to couples, if cohabitation is pervasive and increasing, if it is not confined to particular groups and if this situation is accepted by a majority of the population. How far policy-makers should engage with cohabitation, and whether or not (and if so how) we change the law in response, is to a large degree dependent upon the extent of cohabitation, and the nature of people's attitudes towards it.

This chapter examines these issues, drawing primarily on the findings of the British Social Attitudes survey carried out in 2000 (the BSA survey). We begin by exploring the scope of cohabitation and the characteristics of cohabitants themselves, outlining the sort of people who cohabit and how they compare with married people. We then consider how attitudes to marriage and cohabitation have changed over time, highlighting how views about these two forms of relationship vary from one group to another. Overall we find that people's views of cohabitation and marriage have indeed changed over time. Whilst there is diversity of opinion, marriage has lost much of its social significance and cohabitation is increasingly practised and accepted. It is now more common for people to accept cohabitation as an alternative and a prelude to marriage, as traditional functions of the family (such as sexual intimacy, parenting and companionship) are no longer viewed as the exclusive domain of married couples.

2 WHO COHABITS?

Marriages in Britain are currently at their lowest level since 1917 and the divorce rate is one of the highest in the European Union (National Statistics, 2004). Conversely, heterosexual cohabitation increased dramatically from 5 per cent to 15 per cent of all couples between 1986 and 1999 (Shaw and Haskey, 1999). More recent statistics suggest that 29 per cent of non-married women aged under 60 were cohabiting in 2001/02, almost three times the rate found in 1986. Furthermore, over a quarter of all children were born to cohabiting families by the turn of the century (National Statistics, 2004).

At the time of the BSA survey in 2000, nine per cent of respondents were cohabiting and a further 25 per cent had done so at some point in the past. As Table 2.1 below highlights, cohabiting relationships are most common amongst younger age groups, with 25–34 year olds being the most likely to cohabit and the non-religious being twice as likely to cohabit as the religious. Few elderly couples cohabit and those living in households where the main income source is earnings (as opposed to a pension or benefits) are more likely than others to cohabit.

TABLE 2.1 *Current cohabitation and marriage rates by age, religion and income source*

	% cohabiting	% married	**Base**
All	9	56	*3426*
Age			
18–24	11	4	*277*
25–34	22	44	*614*
35–44	12	64	*715*
45–54	7	70	*521*
55–64	2	78	*501*
65+	1	55	*791*
Religion			
Church of England	7	63	*1039*
Catholic	8	55	*331*
Other Christian	5	59	*560*
Non-Christian	2	56	*132*
No religion	14	49	*1344*
Income source			
Earnings	13	61	*1057*
Pension	1	60	*821*
Benefits	7	30	*213*
Other	1	27	*110*

Source: BSA survey, 2000.

The study did not reveal a significant difference in the educational and social class background of cohabitants and married couples, contradicting views that cohabitants are made up of a socially excluded 'underclass' (see Murray, 1994 and Morgan, 1999). In fact the BSA survey shows that those whose main income is derived from benefits are *less* likely than others to cohabit, and that cohabitants are more qualified than those who do not cohabit.

In the BSA survey we also examined the nature of cohabiting relationships (see also chapter 4), focusing particularly on their duration and whether they tended to be a prelude to marriage rather than a long-term partnership. A popular measure of the strength of a relationship is its duration (although, of course, this does not necessarily follow). Certainly, the average duration of a cohabiting relationship is shorter than that found for marriages, although this is largely a function of the younger average age of cohabitants compared to married spouses (see chapter 4). However, research suggests that the average duration of cohabiting relationships is getting longer (Haskey, 2001) and the BSA survey found that the mean duration among current cohabitants was six and a half years (the median duration was four years). Few cohabitants (only one in five) had been in their relationship for a year or less.

Many cohabiting relationships do lead to marriage, with 59 per cent of past cohabitants in 2000 having gone on to marry each other. However, many of these cohabiting relationships are not just short-lived 'trial marriages', but are rather part of a long movement from dating, through cohabitation, to marriage. This rather undermines the assumption often made that cohabiting relationships are necessarily short-lived and fragile (eg Ermisch, 2002; Ermisch and Franscesconi, 1999). Indeed, the increase in the longevity of cohabiting relationships suggests that, for many, cohabitation is viewed as a realistic alternative to, or a variety of, marriage, taking on many of the attributes and roles of marriage-type relationships. This view is supported by the fact that just over 36 per cent of current cohabitants have been married before, compared to just 19 per cent of married couples. In addition, 42 per cent of the current cohabiting couples interviewed in the BSA survey had had a child together, highlighting how for many, one of the main traditional functions of marriage—parenting—is now also an important element of the cohabiting relationship.

The nature of cohabitants' relationships was explored further in the follow-up interviews where the cohabitants clearly identified themselves as being little different to married couples (see chapter 4). Many felt they were already viewed in the same way as married couples, especially where children were involved. So Angela, cohabiting for 13 years, commented on how her partner's family had accepted her as the 'other half' and how her partner's mum called her 'daughter in law'. She stated categorically that 'there's nothing more I could get being married than what I've got now, nothing whatsoever'. Melanie (who had, at the time of interview, been cohabiting with her partner for ten years, and had two children from a previous relationship living with them) put it like this: 'I think the majority of people do see living together as being as serious as being married, especially if they've got children'. Meanwhile, Susan (who had been with her partner, with whom she had a young son, for three years) said: 'I think they just assume that we're married, they don't know that we actually aren't'. Kevin, who had been cohabiting with his partner for five years at the time of interview, felt the same way, and highlighted how his own perception of people was not premised upon their marital status:

> Within a few feet of this house ... there's a few couples, maybe a dozen more, but I don't even think of them as being not married or whatever, it doesn't even cross my mind—they are together as a couple and that's the way it is.

Indeed, our cohabiting couples generally experienced the same challenges of everyday family life as married couples. Sharon, a cohabitant of seven years with three children (two together and one from a previous relationship), remarked, 'I think that if you're living together you've still got bills together!' Duncan, who lived with his partner and her three children, bemoaned the seemingly inevitable 'transport problem' experienced by all parents:

> ... we are taking kids all over the place at the moment, we just try and share that—I took the kids this morning, Allison picked up the kids tonight and I took them to piano ...

This reality of life for cohabiting couples was summarised succinctly by Angela, cohabiting for 13 years with one child:

> Even though you haven't just took that ceremony and got married, you've still got all the same commitments and you've still got all the pressures.

More people are cohabiting, and for longer, and whilst for many this eventually leads to marriage, others clearly see their relationship as an alternative to, or variety of, marriage. Cohabiting couples are having and raising children and 'behaving' more like married couples and vice versa (see chapter 4). Maybe, as many of the interviews suggested, the very question of whether someone is married or not is becoming irrelevant to everyday practice.

3 ATTITUDES TOWARDS COHABITATION AND MARRIAGE

People's choice of family structure has clearly changed over the last few decades and these changes have been accompanied by changing attitudes towards marriage and cohabitation amongst the general population. The following section highlights these changes and suggests that, whilst there are—as one might expect in any diverse society—differences of opinion, the majority of the British population accept cohabitation as a valid choice for couples and parents.

Cohabitation

By 2000, 67 per cent of the British population agreed with the statement 'it is all right for a couple to live together without intending to get married'. This acceptance of cohabitation was confirmed by a more recent nationwide poll, conducted for BBC One's Panorama programme (broadcast on 24 November 2003), which asked if it was acceptable for couples to live together without getting married. More than four out of five (84 per cent) said it was acceptable to cohabit, with just 12 per cent saying it was wrong.

The younger generation hold particularly liberal attitudes as the fact that 84 per cent of 18 to 24 year olds agreed that 'it is all right for a couple to live together without intending to get married' suggests. However, although older groups remain less accepting of cohabitation, their views have shifted markedly over time. This is illustrated in Table 2.2 below, which shows how, for example, while only 45 per cent of those aged 55 to 64 agreed with cohabitation in 1994, by 2000 57 per cent of that age group agreed.

TABLE 2.2 *Per cent who agree that 'it is all right for a couple to live together without intending to get married', by age, 1994 and 2000*

% who agree	1994	*Base*	2000	*Base*	Change 2000/1989
Age					
18–24	83	*78*	84	*225*	1
25–34	82	*238*	80	*541*	−2
35–44	81	*174*	78	*632*	−3
45–54	62	*160*	75	*470*	+13
55–64	45	*134*	57	*452*	+12
65+	24	*199*	35	*656*	+11

Source: BSA survey, 2000.

Over half the respondents in 2000 went further still: rather than simply tolerate cohabitation, they actively felt that it was a 'good idea' for couples to live together before they got married. This suggests that cohabitation, for many, is viewed as part of the 'natural progression' to marriage and even an essential stage in the development of any long-term relationship. According to Haskey, nearly three quarters of those cohabiting expected to marry each other, and seven out of eight expected to marry at some point (Haskey, 2001: 12). Cohabitants were also asked if they thought there were 'any advantages in living as a couple rather being married'—40 per cent of men and 47 per cent of women agreed that there were advantages and, of those, 51 per cent of men and 43 per cent of women mentioned the idea of a trial marriage (Haskey, 2001; 7). This positive view of cohabitation as a 'trial marriage' was also expressed by a number of interviewees in our follow-up interviews, and is explored further in chapter 4.

Attitudes towards cohabitation among the, albeit small, group of eight African-Caribbean interviewees reflected the BSA findings, with near unanimous support for the statement 'it is all right for a couple to live together without intending to get married' and 'it is a good idea for a couple who intend to get married to live together first'. Attitudes of the Asian interviewees were more traditional. While these views can be seen as reflecting a remaining importance of 'external' religious mores, we should note that fully eight of the 17 respondents identified themselves as 'non-religious'. The majority felt that cohabitating would always be wrong for them. As 21 year old Sabiha put it:

> It's not a done thing is it? It's not normal. We don't see it as normal, whatever normal is. It's not the done thing.

While some were in favour of cohabitation prior to marriage, most said that they would never consider living with someone themselves. As Mujeeb said:

> Mainly my reason for that, for me, for starters, my religion wouldn't allow it. All of my family and everybody would disagree with it. It's something that I would not even consider.

Even within this small group of Asian interviewees there were three exceptions to this view: Jamal (30), Arshad (24) and Rani (21), all men who did not consider themselves to be religious, felt they would be willing to cohabit as a 'trial marriage', as they thought this would provide an opportunity to get to know the person. This might be a reaction against traditionally arranged marriages. Indeed, Rani thought that views are changing even amongst British Asians: '… people are more lenient—well, my parents are. They wouldn't mind as much, now'. Certainly the interviews also showed that, while most thought that cohabitation was not right for them, many also thought it was acceptable for 'White' society.

Marriage and Parenthood

Views about marriage and parenthood have changed considerably since the BSA survey first researched this area back in 1989. Then, 70 per cent felt that 'people who want children ought to get married'. By 1994, this figure had dropped to 57 per cent, and by 2000 stood at 54 per cent of the population. This overall figure provides a useful barometer of how attitudes have changed over time but masks variations in attitudes between different sectors of the population. For example, as Table 2.3 demonstrates, attitudes towards marriage and parenthood vary markedly between different age groups. Eighty five per cent of those aged 65 or above agree that 'people who want children ought to get married', while only 33 per cent of 18 to 24 year olds hold this view. However, despite this variation in attitudes among different age groups, there has been a general liberalisation of attitudes over time, as the number of people in all age groups who agree with the statement has decreased since 1989.

TABLE 2.3 *'People who want children ought to get married', by age, 1989 and 2000*

% agree	1989	*Base*	2000	*Base*	Change 2000/1989
Age					
18–24	41	*167*	33	*225*	–8
25–34	51	*254*	38	*541*	–13
35–44	65	*248*	36	*632*	–29
45–54	80	*207*	50	*470*	–30
55–64	90	*180*	76	*452*	–14
65+	93	*248*	85	*656*	–8

Source: BSA survey, 2000.

The BSA survey revealed other interesting differences in relation to this issue. For example, whilst there was generally little difference of opinion between men and women, young women held more liberal attitudes than young men (only 29 per cent of women aged 18–24 thought marriage should precede parenthood, compared with 39 per cent of young men). Unsurprisingly, religious and married people were more traditional, as were those with no qualifications. However, as Table 2.4 shows, it is notable that those with higher educational qualifications were *more* traditional than those with qualifications at a lower level, going against the general tendency for those with higher qualifications to be more liberal than average (Park, 2000). Nonetheless, even the most traditional groups have become less convinced that marriage should precede parenthood over time. For instance, while 73 per cent of Catholic respondents in 1989 agreed with the statement, only 55 per cent did so in 2000—a drop of 18 percentage points.

In order to further explore attitudes the BSA survey asked a number of detailed questions about marriage and cohabitation. Respondents were asked their views on a number of statements, designed to tease out their beliefs about parenthood and marriage. For example, as reported in Table 2.5, respondents were asked to indicate whether they agreed or disagreed with the view that 'married couples make better parents than unmarried ones'. Only 27 per cent agreed with this statement, suggesting that whilst many (54 per cent) see marriage as an 'ideal' relationship within which to have children, they do not necessarily view unmarried parents as less *able* to raise and care for children. That cohabiting couples with children view themselves as capable parents is also reflected in the follow-up interviews (see chapter 4). The notion that married couples make better parents evoked several heated responses, especially amongst parents. Cohabiting interviewees

TABLE 2.4 *Per cent who agree 'people who want children ought to get married', by sex, education, religion and marital status, 1989 and 2000*

% who agree	1989	Base	2000	Base	Change 2000/1989
By religion					
Church of England	78	476	65	923	−13
Catholic	73	142	55	274	−18
Other Christian	81	185	66	497	−15
No religion	57	447	38	1181	−19
By marital status					
Married	77	833	62	1426	−15
Cohabiting	43	73	23	240	−20
Separated or divorced	52	64	40	370	−12
Widowed	85	98	80	360	−5
Not married	51	205	38	584	−13
By highest educational qualification					
No qualifications	79	534	62	894	−17
CSE/GCSE or equivalent	61	99	48	281	−13
O level/GCSE or equivalent	58	218	47	618	−11
A level or equivalent	57	141	45	319	−12
Higher education below degree	74	162	57	412	−17
Degree	67	111	52	402	−15

Source: BSA survey, 2000.

were particularly annoyed, not because they saw their own parenting skills as ideal, but because they resented the suggestion that couples (and their children) are happier *because* they are married. This suggests that cohabitation, and parenting within it, is not simply something that the British population tolerate, but is increasingly accepted as something similar to marriage (see chapter 4).

As we might expect, given our earlier discussion about Asian attitudes to cohabitation, the Asian interviewees held more traditional views about children and marriage. Their views tended to relate to the perceived instability of a cohabiting relationship (discussed in more detail in chapter 4), and the stigma that their religion attaches to children born out of wedlock. Even Jamal, the only Asian former cohabitant to be interviewed, was ambivalent when it came to his views of the needs of children, despite (or perhaps because of) the fact that he had lived with his partner and fathered a child with her in the past.

> It's alright—it's alright and it's not alright … erm … I'd say it's alright, you know … I say it's alright and it's not alright … I'm like in between there.

Arshad, who was also generally liberal and open minded in his attitude to cohabitation, felt marriage was the best relationship within which to have and raise children:

TABLE 2.5 *Attitudes to marriage and cohabitation*

		Agree	Neither agree nor disagree	Disagree
Married couples make better parents than unmarried ones	%	27	28	43
Even though it might not work out for some people, marriage is still the best kind of relationship	%	59	20	20
Many people who live together without getting married are just scared of commitment	%	36	28	34
Marriage gives couples more financial security than living together	%	48	22	28
There is no point getting married—it's only a piece of paper	%	9	16	73
Too many people just drift into marriage without really thinking about it	%	69	19	10
Base: 2980				

Source: BSA survey, 2000.

> ... 'cos if you're married you're more committed to it. If you're in a marriage, you're committed to your partner—you're committed to your children. Whereas if you're not married, you're just living together as partners—or you're in a common law marriage, you're not as much committed to the partner.

Whilst parenting is still perceived by many as best located within a married partnership (which it is assumed is 'stable, committed and happy'), people's views are shifting to accept those who choose to parent outside the institution of marriage. Certainly an estimated 200,000 children are born annually to cohabiting couples (Hibbs et al, 2001: 203).

Marriage

The BSA survey suggests that marriage is, across the board, still viewed as an 'ideal' type of relationship; only nine per cent dismissed marriage as 'only a piece of paper' and 59 per cent agreed with the statement that marriage is the 'best kind of relationship' (although 40 per cent did not). This ideal view of marriage was also reflected in the in-depth interviews (see chapter 4) and for the Asian interviewees, marriage and commitment were mostly seen as synonymous.

Despite the strength of this ideal notion of marriage, it was generally tempered by a more practical awareness about the efficacy of marriage as an institution for family life. Only a half of respondents in the BSA survey agreed with the statement 'marriage gives couples more financial security than living together', and 69 per cent of respondents agreed that 'too many people drift into marriage without really thinking about it' (Table 2.5).

The overall trends depicted in Table 2.5 mask considerable differences between the sentiments expressed by different groups (and particularly by different age groups). These differences perhaps reflect the fact that cohabitation and marriage have different meanings for different social groups (Manting, 1996 cited in Lewis, 2001; 132). Some differences of view cause particular concern. For example, given that cohabitants can face considerable financial disadvantage when compared to married couples, it is alarming that only 31 per cent of cohabitants agree that 'marriage gives couples more financial security than living together', compared with 50 per cent of married couples. The fact that there were no gender-related differences in views about financial security and marriage is also of concern, given women's overall lower earning power (Rake, 2000), and is perhaps surprising given the traditional view of marriage as a source of financial support for women (Scott et al, 1998).

The differences of opinion expressed by different groups is illustrated particularly well in relation to the statement 'many people who live together without getting married are just scared of commitment'. Overall, just over a third (36 per cent) agreed with this view, and a similar proportion (34 per cent) disagreed. Similar attitudinal differences were also evident when considering the statements about marriage presented in Table 2.4 earlier. Once again, some social groups held more traditional views (older, married, religious, parents, men, non-manual workers and those not in paid work) than others (younger, cohabitants, non-religious, women, manual workers and those in paid work). Many of these characteristics are, of course, related to one another; younger people are less likely to be married than older ones, for example, or to belong to a religion—making it difficult to assess whether it is age, marital status or religion that is most strongly linked to a person's views about marriage. The final section of this chapter explores the implications of these social differences for future attitudes towards cohabitation.

4 EXPLAINING CHANGE IN ATTITUDES

There are a variety of potential reasons why people might hold the particular views they do, and why they make the partnering and parenting choices they do. This is demonstrated by both the BSA survey and the follow-up in-depth interviews. Both show that people's attitudes towards marriage and cohabitation are often subject to marked cultural variations. Similarly, the attributes that we attach to cohabitation and marriage (such as commitment and stability) can differ more between individuals or different social groups, or over time, than between the two forms of the partnership themselves (see also chapter 4). Attitudes and behaviour can, of course, also be influenced by personal experience, as is borne out in a number of the follow-up interviews conducted as part of this study. For instance, experience of poor marriages (which for some included domestic violence) fuelled disillusionment with the institution of marriage (see chapter 4).

Despite these interesting and important individual differences in attitudes towards cohabitation and marriage, the BSA survey demonstrates that we have witnessed a growing acceptance of cohabitation over the past few decades. Across the board there is a sense that cohabitation is now 'here to stay' (Ermisch and Francesconi, 1999). These overall changes of opinion about cohabitation and marriage partly reflect a process of generational change within Britain. As Table 2.2 earlier showed, different age groups have notably different attitudes towards both forms of partnership and, because the young hold more liberal views than older groups and maintain these views as they themselves get older, the dying out of previous, more traditional generations and their replacement by subsequent, more liberal generations is gradually resulting in a shift towards a more liberal view of marriage and cohabitation (Barlow et al, 2001). This points to a strong likelihood that British society will continue to become more liberal on these matters, although particular groups, such as the religious, are likely to remain more traditional than the rest.

Of course, such processes of generational replacement cannot account for all the change we have seen. After all, some of the most dramatic shifts in opinion have occurred among those groups with the most 'traditional' views (the religious, for instance, or older age groups). In 1994, for example, 45 per cent of 55 to 64 year olds thought it acceptable for a couple to live together without intending to get married (Table 2.2); by 2000, 57 per cent of this same age group took that view. This is likely to reflect the growing exposure of different groups within society to cohabitation. As one of our interviewees, Nigel, put it:

> I'm sure there's more acceptance because of more people going the same way, you have to accept that's what's happening.

Melanie Phillips has suggested that, for many, the reason for such tolerant responses to cohabitation is the effect of 'a parental instinct to protect their offspring' who are 'increasingly living together or having children outside of marriage.' According to Phillips, these views are the result of it being 'human nature to make excuses for ones you love, to be concerned for their welfare and reluctant to pass judgements' (Phillips, 2001). At one level, it is the case that it is increasingly common for people to have children outside marriage, and clearly common behaviour patterns will influence attitudes and vice versa (Haskey, 2001: 5). However, it may also be that people are, as Nigel's comment above and the attitudinal analysis through the BSA survey (see Table 2.5) both suggest, *accepting* cohabitation and parenting as a result, rather than merely *tolerating* it as Phillips implies.

This distinction between toleration and acceptance is important. Toleration, as Zygmunt Bauman (1991: 8) describes, is partly a way of 'reaffirming the other's inferiority' or, as Medus (1989: 149) states, implying 'that the thing tolerated is morally reprehensible'. Thus, if the British population were merely tolerating cohabitation, they would, in effect, be reaffirming the superiority of the institution of marriage. This distinction is important because it impacts on how, and whether, the law should be reformed to better reflect people's attitudes (see chapters 5 and 6). If the change in attitudes is simply a reflection of an increasing toleration of unmarried cohabitation, rather than its acceptance, then reform to ensure legal equality between married and cohabiting families would be less justified. However, as our analysis of the BSA survey and the qualitative interviews shows, this is not the case. Unmarried cohabitation is increasingly and widely practised and accepted as a family form.

5 CONCLUSION

Marriage, whilst still viewed as an ideal relationship in the abstract, is no longer viewed as essential, desirable or even practical in 21st century Britain. Similarly, the traditional functions of families (such as sexual intimacy, parenting and companionship) are no longer viewed as the exclusive domain of married couples. Concomitantly, it is now more common for people, especially within younger generations, to practise and accept cohabitation as a variety of, or an alternative to, marriage, and this is accepted by the majority. Even where cohabitation is a temporary arrangement (either as a prelude to marriage or as a way of 'testing' a relationship's strength) it can last quite a long time. It is also increasingly common for children to be born to couples who are cohabiting. Nor are there many educational and social class differences in background of cohabitants and married couples, although cohabiting couples with children are less likely to be in middle-class groups. Consequently, how we depict these families, and whether—and to what extent—we legally protect them has wide social ramifications.

Diversity of opinion is obviously going to persist but policy-makers should not ignore the voice of a growing majority of the population which clearly views cohabitation as one of society's repertoire of permissible family types. And this repertoire has developed 'as people respond creatively to the challenges of everyday living in contexts where some of the older cultural and institutional constraints have lost their bite' (Carling, 2002; 4).

3

The Common Law Marriage Myth and 'Lived Law': An Analysis of Beliefs

1 INTRODUCTION

Informal marriages have not been legally recognised since Lord Hardwicke's Marriage Act was passed by Parliament in 1753 (more fully 'For the better preventing of Clandestine Marriages'). This Act laid the basis for the modern law of marriage by making compliance with prescribed formalities essential to the validity of a marriage. The Act formalised marriage so that they were only legally valid if preceded by a calling of banns (three times in the Parish Church on consecutive Sundays), or if a licence was obtained from a Bishop, and solemnised in a Church. As David Johnson observed, the legislation reflected the 'determination of the drafters to establish total state control over marriage' (Johnson, 2003; 42). Although Rebecca Probert described the 1753 Act as 'part of a gradual progression towards regularity and formality rather than an abrupt shift in the regulation of marriage' (Probert, 2005), it did mean that after 1753 less formal arrangements, including situations where a man and a woman would live together and have children, were no longer recognised by law. Succeeding legislation over the next century or so, starting with the Marriage Act 1836 and the Registration Act 1836, allowed couples to marry outside the Church of England and by civil registration; this relaxed the need for a particular religious ceremony but in so doing maintained the legal regulation and formalisation of marriage. In this way the state imposes its authority on the process of marriage and creates a legal dividing line between marriage and cohabitation (Finch, 2004).

Despite this legal regulation of what could be recognised as marriage, the notion of a legally recognised status of 'common law marriage', together with those of a 'common law husband' or a 'common law wife' have survived to the present day. As this chapter will demonstrate, there is a widely held belief that heterosexual couples living together 'as man and wife' acquire 'marriage-like' rights and responsibilities through 'common law marriage', at least after a given period of time. This is what we call the common law marriage myth. As family lawyers can testify, this 'myth' often surfaces as a deeply held view with detrimental implications for those who believe. However, the exact scope and depth of this myth has been unclear. The 2000 BSA survey, which we draw on here, provided the first representative national information on its extent and nature, and our interview surveys provided further information about cohabitants' understandings of it.

In order to assess the nature of the common law marriage myth, we first have to chart the actual legal situation regarding cohabiting couples. We immediately come across a difficulty, for while British law is clear about the legal status of marriage and the procedures necessary to become married, it is more confused about the legal status of unmarried, cohabiting couples. Indeed, as we shall see later in the chapter, this very legal confusion supports belief in common law marriage. As explained in chapter 1, sometimes unmarried couples are treated the same as married couples, for example for income-related social security benefits and Working Family Tax Credit purposes. At other times, cohabitants are treated quite differently to married couples, for example on relationship breakdown, for inheritance purposes on the death of a partner, where there is no will and in relation to parental responsibility (see chapters 1 and 5). Although civil partnerships for homosexual unions are at the time of writing part of the current government's political agenda, there are no plans to provide a consolidated package of legal rights and responsibilities for unmarried heterosexual couples and their families. Yet, the consequences of believing in common law marriage are often devastating for people's everyday lives and well-being. Worse, because this belief is so deeply held, the damaging consequences of this legal void are often recognised only when it is too late. It is therefore crucial, before we consider whether legal reform is necessary and what shape such reform should take (see chapters 5 and 6), that we assess the extent of the common law marriage myth, and chart what rights people think they acquire through unmarried cohabitation.

2 THE EXTENT OF THE COMMON LAW MARRIAGE MYTH

In the national 2000 BSA survey respondents were asked 'as far as you know do unmarried couples who live together for some time have a "common law marriage" which gives them the same legal rights as married couples?' Only 37 per cent were aware that cohabitants do not have the same legal rights as married couples, while over half of all respondents (56 per cent) believed that cohabitants and married couples are treated equally in law. This evidence clearly shows that belief in common law marriage is widespread in Britain.

We were also able, through the BSA survey, to assess whether this belief is more prevalent in some groups than in others. The survey revealed slight but interesting variations by gender, age and social class. The number of men who thought that common law marriage existed in law (59 per cent) is slightly higher than the number of women (at 54 per cent). Conversely, only 35 per cent of men and 40 per cent of women did not believe this. The most stark difference between men and women was for the under 25 age group, where this gender difference is reversed—only 45 per cent of men, compared to 56 per cent of women, believed in the existence of common law marriage. In general age was not a significant factor in belief/non-belief; over half of all age groups believed that married and unmarried couples have the same legal rights and responsibilities, although the 18–25 age group were slightly more aware of the true legal situation (51 per cent believing and 40 per cent not believing in the myth). Those who were not affiliated to a particular religion were slightly more likely to believe in the existence of common law marriage than those who were. Thus 57 per cent of those with no religious affiliation believed common law marriage existed, and 36 per cent did not. For self identified Christian respondents, 53 per cent believed in this and 42 per cent did not. There was also a slight social class gradient, where those with a degree, and professional workers, were slightly less likely to believe in common law marriage, while those with no qualifications were more likely to believe in its existence (although this group was also older).

The BSA survey was unable (due to respondent numbers) to assess the views of British African-Caribbean or Asian groups. However, this issue was pursued in the interviews, which, although not nationally representative, provides indicative information. Our African-Caribbean interviewees were more aware of the legal differences in the treatment of married and unmarried couples than the respondents in the BSA survey overall; four of the eight African-Caribbean interviewees knew that common law marriage does not exist, with only two believing that it did and two were unsure. The Asian interviewees more closely reflected the BSA findings—seven of the seventeen interviewees thought that common law marriage existed, while four were unsure and six did not believe this.

Regional differences are also minimal, although those living in the North and Midlands of England were more likely to believe in the existence of common law marriage, with 60 and 59 per cent respectively of respondents, compared with 54 per cent in Wales and 52 per cent in the South of England and London. In Scotland, the legal situation is different. Here, 'marriage by habit and repute' (a form of common law marriage) is still legally recognised and, if legally established (a couple must be free to marry, have been cohabiting for long enough for a promise to be inferred and be consistently regarded as married by most other people) means that couples are treated as married in the eye of the law (see Bissett-Johnson and Barton, 1999). This form of common law marriage in Scotland has only very rarely been established, however, and according to the Scottish Social Attitudes Survey (2000) the number of respondents living in Scotland who thought (incorrectly) that unmarried couples automatically have a common law marriage bestowing them with the same legal rights as married couples was, at 57 per cent, slightly higher than in England and Wales (see Barlow, 2000).

It might be expected that those most likely to be subject to legal penalties, or to gain legal rights, would be more aware of the true legal situation than average. This was not the case—if anything the opposite was true. Thus, although parental rights and responsibilities differ for cohabiting and married fathers, 59 per cent of parents (married or unmarried, single or cohabiting) believed that common law marriage existed and only 36 per cent did not. Similarly 59 per cent of the current cohabitants surveyed (with and without children) believed in the existence of common law marriage compared to only 35 per cent who correctly stated that it did not exist. Those most likely to be detrimentally affected by incorrect belief in common law marriage—cohabiting parents—are even more likely to believe in its existence. Similarly in one study of 173 couples in Cheshire and Staffordshire who were engaged to be married, 69 per cent of those cohabiting thought that living together unmarried had legal consequences (Hibbs et al, 2001). Conversely, the same research found that

> 41 per cent of all respondents thought marriage would not change the legal nature of their relationship with their partner, and 37 per cent thought that it would not have legal consequences for them with regard to their present or future children (Hibbs et al, 2001: 201).

In an earlier study, conducted in Merthyr Tydfil in South Wales and Great Yarmouth in Norfolk (Barlow and Duncan, 2000), nearly all of the thirty mothers interviewed wrongly believed that cohabitants had the same rights as married couples in relation to pensions or other allowances, maintenance and claims for a share in property on separation.

The overall message from the national BSA survey is that belief in the legal existence of common law marriage is not only a majority position in Britain, but pervades all social groups, and is not concentrated to any particular age, class, sex or region. The in-depth interviews illustrate this well. For instance Caroline, a 22 year old from Nottingham, had been living with her partner (a welder) and their two young sons for five years at the time of the interview. Caroline said that she had always classed herself 'as his common-law wife.' Mathew, a 51 year old, divorced Systems Tester in Doncaster, who'd lived with his partner (and their two children) for 20 years before they married in 1997, also believed in the common law marriage myth. So did Angela, a 37 year old Store Manager from Birmingham, who'd been living with her partner (and their son) for 13 years at the time of interview. She believed that the law protects her in the same way as it protects married couples—as she put it:

> Oh yes definitely, the same yes ... if it did go wrong I know that half of everything is mine and half my partner's. Oh yes, you've got the same legal rights.

On the other hand 'non-believers' came from equally diverse backgrounds. They included Mary, a 42 year old Manager, who lived in Northampton with her partner, his 12 year old daughter (from a previous relationship) and their two year old daughter. They had been cohabiting for nine years at the time of interview. Another 'non-believer', Kevin, a 45 year old Engineer from Ebbw Vale, had been cohabiting for five years at the time of the interview. He had a daughter with his current partner and although not aware of the details he thought that there are some differences in the legal treatment of married and unmarried couples: As he put it:

> I know some people think that if you live together continuously for x amount of time you were considered to be common-law man and wife etc ... but the legal ramifications I don't know—I've never really looked at it or thought about it—I know there are a lot of misconceptions about it ...

In a similar vein, Sophie, a 27 year old cohabitant of two and half years, living in Shrewsbury, was aware that there is a difference but, despite this knowledge, still used the terminology 'common law wife':

> You don't have as many rights—you don't have the same rights as a married couple—you're not joined by law as it were, are you? I know I'm classed as a common-law wife but I haven't got the same rights as a married lady.

This suggests that self-labelling does not necessarily reflect a person's legal knowledge, and points to the existence of common law marriage as 'lived law' in a social world outside formal law.

In 2000, a majority of the British public believed that married and unmarried couples have the same legal rights and responsibilities, and this belief was pervasive among all social groups and geographical areas. However, we still need to know whether there a commonality of belief, or whether 'common law marriage' means different things to different people. We also need to know what impact (if any) these understandings have on behaviour, and where and how people acquire their beliefs. The in-depth interviews in combination with the BSA survey allowed us to explore these questions.

3 THE NATURE OF THE COMMON LAW MARRIAGE MYTH

Initially the BSA 2000 survey suggested a three-way categorisation of people's belief in the legal existence of common law marriage—into 'believers', 'non-believers' and the 'unsure'. The 'believers' were, we assumed, unaware of any of the legal consequences of cohabiting outside marriage: 56 per cent of the BSA respondents fell into this category. The 'non-believers' had, we assumed, a reasonably clear view of the actual legal situation: 37 per cent of respondents fitted this definition. Finally, a small third group—just six per cent—were unsure of the legal position. These respondents, we assumed, were more closely affiliated to the non-believers than the believers as their uncertainty probably reflected the confused and ad-hoc character of the legal framework. Extending this classification to the in-depth interviews, seventeen of the 48 follow-up interviewees, with nine of the 28 minority ethnic group interviews held the first 'believer' position, apparently unaware of the actual legal position, while twenty and twelve respectively of the two samples held the second apparently more knowledgeable, 'non-believer' position. Finally, eleven and six respectively took the third, more confused, 'unsure' position. This categorisation is neatly depicted in Table 3.1:

TABLE 3.1: *Belief in Common Law Marriage*

	'Believers'	'Non-believers'	'Unsure'	Total
BSA survey	56%	37%	6%	2980
Follow-up interviews	17	20	11	48
Minority ethnic group interviews	9	12	6	28

Source: BSA survey, 2000, follow up interviews 2001.

However, the qualitative interview analysis showed that this simple categorisation disguises the complex nature of the common law marriage myth as it is experienced in people's everyday lives. There was considerable diversity in people's understandings and misunderstandings of the legal framework, and this blurred the distinction between those whom we classified as legally aware, and those we categorised as unaware. In addition, we found that beliefs are not necessarily static; even in the short time between the BSA survey and the follow-up interview several respondents had changed their opinion of how the law operates. Like other research (Ewick and Silbey, 1992), this shows that legal consciousness can vary with time.

One important instant of this blurring was the diversity of opinion between interviewees of when the assumed 'legal rights' of common law marriage come into effect. Of the 17 believers, seven thought that such rights accrued immediately on co-residence, while ten thought they commenced after a given period of time cohabiting. This time varied from six months to six years; five believed that such rights commenced after less than a year cohabiting, while the other five thought the rights began once a couple had been cohabiting for between 2–3 years (two of the ten) or 5–6 years (three of the ten). Amanda, for example, who at the time of the interview had lived with her partner for seven years, believed that:

> … You have to be living together for six months and then everything gets split down the middle.

Natasha had lived with her partner for 17 years at the time of interview. They rented a council house (in both their names) in south London and had no legal provisions in place. But according to her,

> ... the law says providing you've lived together for 18 months–2 years, you have the same rights as a married couple so if we were to split up he's entitled to half of whatever's in this house and I'm entitled to half. You can't say half the house is his because it's not ours. The law says half is his, half is mine, again, if you're married it's exactly the same—half of everything ...

Similarly, Hibbs and colleagues (2001) found that while most of the respondents in their study thought cohabitants acquired rights after a varying amount of time, six months was the most popular.

The interviews also allowed us to delve deeper into the specifics of the individual's legal knowledge. Most, understandably, lacked confidence in their responses at this point, and unless they had particular legal knowledge (usually based on their own experience of the law), were cautious and eager to emphasise that they were stating assumptions about what they thought the law would do in the given situation. We also found that respondents who confidently expressed a belief that married and cohabiting couples are treated equally in law in a general sense subsequently lost conviction in their original statement when it came to particular legal issues. Their ability to define how common law actually operated was flawed. This suggests that the social meaning of common law marriage is general rather than specific. We will consider this further by looking in turn at the specific areas of children, tax and social security, pensions, maintenance and inheritance.

Children: Cohabiting Fathers

In 2000 unmarried fathers were not automatically given parental responsibility for their children in the way that married fathers are when birth is registered (Children Act 1989 s2). They had to make a formal parental responsibility agreement with the mother or obtain an order from the court (Children Act 1989 s4). The law changed with the enactment of s111 of the Adoption and Children Act 2002 in December 2003, which gives parental responsibility to unmarried fathers who attend with the mother to jointly register the birth of their child. However, this new right for unmarried fathers is not retrospective—nor is it automatic as joint attendance is required rather than, as with married fathers, simply naming by the mother. How far are people aware of this aspect of unmarried cohabitation?

In the BSA survey all respondents were asked whether they thought an unmarried, and cohabiting, father had the same legal rights and responsibilities as a married father using a specific scenario. We asked:

> Now imagine an unmarried couple who have been living together for ten
> years. They have a child who needs medical treatment. Do you think the
> father does in fact have the same rights as a married man to make decisions
> about his child's medical treatment as he would if he was married to the
> child's mother?

Fifty per cent of all respondents incorrectly thought that the cohabiting father had,
in this situation, the same rights as a married father. Thirty-eight per cent thought
(correctly) that he did not have the same rights as a married father and 12 per cent
were unsure.

This issue was explored further in the in-depth interviews both directly and
through the same scenario question, and this allows us to explore people's reasoning behind their beliefs. Twenty-three year old Claire from Leeds provided a
good example of the 'unaware' believer position. She did not have any children
of her own at the time of interview, and assumed that legal rights and responsibilities towards children would not depend on marital status, but rather on the fact
of parentage. As she put it:

> I'd say that they do have the same rights and responsibilities. … I would pre-
> sume that they do. I can't see why they couldn't because if there's a child
> involved and the couple live together I would say that marriage shouldn't
> make a difference really to the legal rights of that child or the child's parents.

Similarly, Martin, from London, who cohabited with his partner and their young
daughter, took the same view. As he said:

> I would say yes because you're still parents—whether you're married or not
> is irrelevant—you're still the parents of the child. I think as far as the law is
> concerned then yes, the same rights and responsibilities.

Indeed, nearly all the interviewees who were asked to consider the scenario question regarding medical treatment thought that the father would have the right to
consent to medical treatment, and that this particular right would be available
from the birth of the child—regardless of how long the couple had been living
together. So for Amanda, who thought that cohabiting couples gained legal equality with married couples after six months of cohabiting, this worked as an exception to her general understanding of the law:

> Yeah, because at the end of the day it doesn't matter whether they've been
> together a year or two years. It's still their child, isn't it?

Here, parenting as a moral position was assumed to veto contract based rights.

Most of the interviewees who thought that fathers obtained parental responsibility by virtue of being the child's father agreed with Amanda; they thought such
rights did not depend on the couple cohabiting for any particular period of time.

For some, as with Amanda, this worked as an 'exception' to their general understanding of common law marriage. More rarely, this exceptioning also moved in the opposite direction. Thus Caroline, who overall believed in the existence of common law marriage, was a 'non-believer' in relation to this issue. Interestingly, her belief was based on her own experience—she knew that the father did not have the right to consent to medical treatment because she had actually been in that situation—although this did not mean she thought it was right:

> ... the nurse was asking us questions and she ... said to him 'you can leave because it doesn't concern you, the decision isn't yours'. I was like, oh my god and his face just dropped as if to say 'I've got no rights—no decision of his well-being where medical treatment is concerned'—it was all down to me and I think it's so wrong.

Hence, in relation to this specific issue, individuals appear to move between the three static categories outlined above of those who are legally unaware, legally knowledgeable and those who are more sceptical and unsure. An idea that the law should sensibly reflect the moral rights and responsibilities of fathers, rather than be based on contractual or formal relations, seemed influential here. Certainly, only a minority of the British population are aware of the legal disempowering of cohabiting fathers. As an estimated 200,000 children were born annually to cohabiting couples by the turn of the century, and this is expected to increase substantially (Haskey, 2001), this provides some cause for concern.

Children: Registration of the Birth

The registration of the birth and the naming of the father on the birth certificate cannot of itself confer any legal rights or responsibilities on the unmarried father. As stated above, this has partially changed with the enactment of the Adoption and Children Act 2002 in December 2003, in that parental rights now accrue to a father who jointly registers. However, this is not retrospective nor is it automatic, as with married fathers. The in-depth interviews again revealed a considerable lack of awareness about this. Interviewees were asked whether they thought the registration of the birth had any legal affect on parental rights and responsibilities. Sixteen of the 48 interviewees incorrectly believed (for the 2000 situation) that it did. For example, Mary, who was originally classified as a more knowledgeable 'non-believer', was unaware of the true legal situation concerning registration. Living in Northampton with her partner of nine years, their two year-old daughter and 12 year old stepdaughter, she thought that simply naming the father on the birth certificate gave him parental rights. This is as incorrect post the 2002 Act as in 2000. Similarly, Judy, who lived in Cheltenham with her partner of 17 years and their two children, knew that generally speaking cohabitants and married couples are treated differently in law, but in relation to this issue thought incorrectly that:

... if you've got both parents on there then they have got a legal right to the
child, yes.

Lynda was also a 'knowledgeable' interviewee overall but was unsure of the legal
ramifications of registering the birth. She had been living with her partner in
Crawley for over eight years at the time of interview and had a five year old and
a three year old together. According to her:

Yes, if he was on the birth certificate I would think he does but if his name
was not on the birth certificate, then probably not, you'd probably have to
have some stupid signed Agreement or something.

Angela too assumed that her partner of 13 years had some parental rights and
responsibility for their 12 year old son, and assumed that the birth certificate con-
ferred these rights:

I don't know, I should say so. If you look at it logical it's got to do but I don't
really know.

Angela, like the others discussed here, was originally classified as a non-believer
(or legally 'knowledgeable') interviewee. Overall 15 of the 17 'non-believers' in
the follow-up interviews were in fact unsure or incorrect about how registration
at birth affects the father's legal rights. Previous research confirms this result,
where most respondents assume automatic parental rights for fathers are a consequence of being named as father on registration of the birth (Barlow and Duncan,
2000; Pickford, 1999; Smart and Stevens, 2000). As with fathers' parental rights
in general, belief in the legal existence of common law marriage seems to be even
more extensive when it comes to registration of birth as a means of gaining these
rights. Again, this widespread belief in the legal basis of common law marriage
seems to be based on what appears to respondents as 'logical' and morally correct for fathers and their children.

Children: Parental Responsibility Agreements/Orders

Very few cohabiting parents arrange parental responsibility orders or agreements
through which the father's parental rights can be assured. While not directly concerning common law marriage, widespread use would indicate a lack of belief in
its legal efficacy. But the opposite was the case: the BSA survey shows that in
2000 only five per cent of current cohabitants with children had a parental responsibility agreement or order in place. In the follow-up interviews we asked whether
the respondent had even heard of a parental responsibility agreement or order—
only three of the 48 had done, and held some understanding of what this was. And
only a single respondent had actually taken out an agreement. Hibbs and colleagues (2001) report a similar result in their study of 173 engaged couples. The

three respondents who had heard about parental responsibility orders had done so through friends and family, or through accidental 'legal' experience. Melanie had heard about them through a friend's experience following an accident where consent to medical treatment was needed, Gail realised how useful these could be after visiting a solicitor about another related issue and Susan—the one exception who actually had a parental responsibility agreement—had received (and acted upon) advise from her sister, a probation officer.

Other interviewees thought they had heard of parental responsibility agreements/orders but it transpired during the interview that they thought these applied only when the relationship broke down or when problems occurred. For example, Naomi, a cohabitant of 15 years with two children, described it as 'a legal responsibility thing ... like a crisis thing rather than something you would just do'. Alex, a cohabitant of two years with a young daughter, thought that it was 'an order made by social services for some sort of responsibility.'

This dearth of knowledge about parental responsibility orders or agreements, and their almost complete lack of use, goes along with what we have discovered so far about the common law marriage myth and children. In this area, the myth is even more pervasive and deeply held, apparently because people imagine that the law would be 'logical' and 'moral' in recognising fathers' parental rights. Unfortunately, this is not the case.

Tax and Social Security

Confusingly, while most of the law treats unmarried cohabitants and married persons differently, the law relating to tax and social security largely treats them as the same. Married and unmarried couples are treated in the same way for the purpose of means-tested and income based benefits and while married couples used to enjoy tax advantages in relation to income tax, this is no longer the case—although there still are differences in relation to capital gains tax (see Barlow, 2001). The 31 interviewees who replied that that they did not believe in the legal existence of common law marriage, or were unsure, were asked whether they thought the law relating to tax and welfare benefits favours married as opposed to unmarried couples with children. Sixteen (incorrectly) thought that it did, eight (correctly) thought that it did not and seven were unsure or gave no answer. Hence half of the initially 'knowledgeable' non-believers and the 'sceptic' unsure respondents did not realise that the law treats unmarried couples in the same way for the purposes of tax and welfare benefits. For example, Sophie, a cohabitant of two and a half years with no children, thought that mothers who cohabit would be classed as lone mothers:

> I think it favours unmarried couples because you get your child benefit, family tax credit—I would say there was definitely more benefits for unmarried mothers than there would be for married mothers because obviously if they're married they've got the stability of their partner, husband ...

Others rather thought that married people would gain; thus Jane (cohabiting for ten years) simply believed that:

> ... they are treated differently. I think it's more in favour of married people.

While Duncan, a teacher cohabiting for five years, was perhaps remembering the earlier situation when he claimed that the law

> ... favours married couples in terms of the tax grading of couples, it's a better married person's allowance than it is two single allowances as far as I remember.

Again, the interviews exposed further complexities of the common law marriage myth. In this case many of the original 'knowledgeable non-believers' incorrectly extend this position to the very case where cohabitants and married spouses do receive largely equal treatment. Ironically, the law surrounding tax and benefits has been changed to a more 'logical' position, whereby similar family economic units are treated similarly. But this legal exception creates all the more confusion. We might also note the fact that where the economic interests of the state are concerned, legal reform to equate cohabiting and married couples has taken place—strange how similar reforms are seen as less possible or desirable when it is the economic interests of weaker family members, usually mothers and children, which are at stake.

Pensions

Cohabitants are treated differently from married couples in relation to state pension entitlement (see Barlow, 2001). We asked the same 31 'knowledgeable non-believers' and 'sceptic' interviewees whether they thought unmarried couples got the same state pension rights as married couples: four thought they did, 14 thought they did not and 13 were unsure or did not answer. Many of the interviewees were vague and/or unwilling to commit to an answer and it transpired that the majority were not sure what the situation was either for married *or* unmarried couples, rather than simply a lack of knowledge about the legal situation for cohabitants. For example, Patricia, a former cohabitant, living in Cardiff with her son from that relationship, reflected this general uncertainty. She:

> ... didn't realise that pensions were done as couples anyway. I thought pensions were always individual, I didn't think they would change if you were a couple or not but I don't know ...

Sally, a former cohabitant living in Havant with her son, was also unsure of the legal situation in relation to pensions but thought that it would 'probably be similar'. She justified her conclusion on the grounds that:

> ... at the end of the day we're all the same aren't we?—just because you've
> got a certificate to say you're married or you haven't, you're still all people and
> all need the same sort of needs in life. So I think it would be pretty similar.

Again we see that people tend to assume that the law will reflect what seems to
them to be logically and morally sensible from the point of view of families,
whereas the current law starts from a different premise. Given the rise in the number of older couples cohabiting (Haskey, 2001) this uncertainty about the legal
situation vis-à-vis pensions is of concern. In this case legal uncertainty gains an
extra twist: people are not only misinformed about the status of common law marriage, but about pension rights in general.

Maintenance Post-Separation

Ex-cohabiting couples cannot claim for maintenance post-separation in the same
way as separated spouses. In order to investigate people's awareness of this different legal treatment, respondents in the national survey were asked to consider
the following scenario:

> I'd now like you to imagine an unmarried couple with no children who have
> been living together for ten years. Say their relationship ends. Do you think
> the woman ... does in fact have the same rights as a married woman to claim
> financial support from the man, or does she have fewer rights?

In the BSA study, over half, 54 per cent, of all respondents correctly thought
that a woman in this situation would have fewer rights than a married woman
(38 per cent believed that she has the same rights, and eight per cent did not
know). All interviewees in the follow-up in-depth study (either explicitly or in
the form of the same scenario question) were asked whether or not they thought
unmarried couples have the same legal responsibilities as married couples when
a relationship breaks down. Seventeen thought that they did, 22 thought not,
and nine were unsure or did not answer. For this issue, then, belief in the legal
efficacy of supposed common law marriage was less pervasive, if still widespread.

The interviews showed that some people think that the right to claim maintenance depended on how long a couple had been together. For example, Claire,
single and living in Leeds following a period of six months cohabiting at the time
of interview, thought that:

> you have had to be living together for so many years ... Is it two years? I
> think it's two years, well that's what I've heard.

This idea of time together as creating eligibility for rights reflects ideas on when
common law marriage rights as a whole are believed to commence (see above).

Other respondents introduced qualifications concerning employment and financial contributions, so according to 38 year old Melanie, who'd been cohabiting for ten years at the time of interview:

> I suppose it does depend on how much they've been living together and whether she's actually worked during the relationship or whether she's just at home and all that sort of thing.

Similarly, Hibbs and colleagues (2001) found that many thought that in sharing household expenses cohabitants acquired property rights; 43 per cent of the men and women in their sample who had moved into their partner's home thought they had acquired a claim and 66 per cent of all their respondents thought that such a right arose from living together. Here again, respondents appear to be following a judgement of what seems to be logically and morally sensible.

Inheritance

Here the law adds to the confusion by partially treating cohabitants like spouses. In the event of a partner dying and having not made a will, a spouse will automatically inherit from his/her partner. Cohabitants may (since 1996) apply for financial provision if they had been living together for over two years but this award is limited and less favourable than the provisions available for a spouse.

The need for cohabitants to make a will is therefore very important in this context. The BSA survey findings suggest that, unfortunately, very few actually do so: only ten per cent of past or present cohabitants and 14 per cent of current cohabitants had made a will that reflected their cohabitant status. To discover whether respondents were aware of the different treatment of unmarried and married couples on death, the BSA survey asked the following scenario question:

> Imagine another unmarried couple without children who have been living together for ten years and live in a house bought in the man's name. Say he dies without making a will. Do you think the woman ... does in fact have the same rights as a married woman to remain in this home, or, does she have fewer rights?

Over a third, 37 per cent, incorrectly thought that she had the right to the family home after the death of her partner, ten per cent were unsure and 53 per cent correctly thought that she did not have that right. As with maintenance, belief in the legal powers of common law marriage are less widespread, if still common.

Interviewees in the follow-up study were also asked (again, either explicitly or using the scenario above) what they thought would happen to the property of a cohabitant were s/he to die. Their answers point to the reasoning behind their beliefs. For example Diane, a 26 year old cohabitant of one year at the time of interview, thought inheritance rights related to the number of years the couple had been together:

I think she could because it's been ten years—if he dies I know it's under his
name but the law should let her. … It could be four or it could be three but I
think after five years that is the main point.

This again reflects the time eligibility concept for common law marriage in general. Again, for property linked rights belief in common law marriage is less
widespread and, when believed, less favourable to cohabitants than for rights surrounding parenting.

This exploration of the particular legal situations of relevance to cohabiting
couples suggests a multi-layering of belief in common law marriage. At the
first general level a majority of the British public believe that common law
marriage exists, giving cohabitants the same rights as married couples. In a
legal sense this majority are, at this general level, legally 'unaware'. A large
minority, however, do not believe in the myth and can therefore be seen as
legally 'aware', while some remain unsure or sceptical of the true legal situation. A second layer for the 'believers' concerns time eligibility; some believe
common law marriage is triggered on the day a couple move in together and
others believe this occurs after a period of time, ranging from six months to six
years. As we have seen, this notion of time eligibility spills over into ideas
about income and property rights, such as maintenance and inheritance.
However, rights and duties concerning children are seen as less time based.
The third layer of belief relates to specific legal issues and here belief in the
legal effects of common law marriage contracts and expands. For issues where
children are involved, the common law marriage myth is more pervasive and
deeply held, while for property issues belief in the legal status of common law
marriage is somewhat less widespread, and—where believed—is seen as less
favourable to cohabitants.

This layering is perhaps not surprising when the law is itself confusing and contradictory. In addition, people tend to assume that the law will reflect what they see
as socially logical and morally sensible in supporting families, while also being fair
to individuals. The more vague answers by interviewees provided good illustrations
of this. For example, 24 year old Patricia's legal understanding was based, in her
words, on 'something that I feel should be', and hence she thought that cohabitants
gained legal rights on a par with married couples after five years of living together.
On the other hand, Craig, a 57 year old cohabitant of six years, believed that on the
whole cohabitants have fewer rights than married couples. This was based on his
beliefs of what he saw as the 'logical' situation, claiming that any other outcome
would be 'totally illogical'. Others relied on their 'gut feeling' (Sandra) or 'general concept' of what they thought law is like (Tony). This moral view of what the
law ought to be helps to explain the high rates of belief in marriage like rights for
cohabitants where children and fathering is concerned, but lower—and often time
restricted—rights for income and property. The law, however, does not follow this
logic at all consistently.

How, then, do people acquire their own sense of what common law marriage means? There are two levels in answering this question: where people find information and how they evaluate this information. The next two sections will go on to look at these questions in turn.

4 ACQUIRING INFORMATION ABOUT COMMON LAW MARRIAGE

We asked interviewees about their sources of legal information in the follow-up survey. Generally, the results point to an informal knowledge world where most respondents get the bulk of their information from friends and family. For example, Emily, a cohabitant of five years who generally believed in common law marriage, saw friends as a major source of information as it was 'just one of the things that has come up in conversation, like from friends who have been living together'. Caroline, also a cohabitant of five years, also pinpointed everyday conversations as the source of her understanding common law marriage but traced this back to her childhood:

> When I was a kid. Listening to adult conversations between my mum and she'd be talking to her mates saying she was living together and I've been living with him for so many years now, I'm his common-law wife and that's where I heard it from. It's as you get older you learn more about what things mean but I do class myself as a common-law wife. I don't use it to other people like 'Oh I'm a common-law wife', I call him my partner ...

Sally, who was single at the time of the interview but who had been in a short-term cohabiting relationship in the past, was a 'non-believer' and was therefore generally aware that there is a difference in the general treatment of married and unmarried. She also mainly obtained her information from talking to friends. As she put it:

> No, it's just at times when I've gone through bad patches I've sat and spoken to my friends and things like that—you get chatting and they say 'Well, you've got the rights to do this'... I suppose I've learnt a lot like that.

Jessica, a cohabitant for 11 years with two daughters at the time of interview, knew that married and unmarried couples are treated differently for inheritance purposes but thought that they are otherwise treated the same, at least after six months of cohabiting. Her personal understanding of the law therefore differs again but it too is rooted in everyday conversations with friends and colleagues:

> Yes, just friends and colleagues at work, yes, it's what you pick up from listening to people.

What an individual believes about common law marriage seems to depend largely upon the knowledge in their particular social network, rather than more formal sources of information. Indicatively, any professional legal advice was mostly relayed through these informal networks of family and friends who were lawyers or otherwise professionally engaged, rather than formally. Thus Mary found out about the importance of making a will when you are not married from an ex-boyfriend who was a solicitor. Naomi found out about the parental responsibility agreements and orders from her sister who worked as a legal executive. Overall, a dominant idea seems to be that you see a solicitor if things go wrong and even then this is to be avoided if at all possible. For example, Richard had married his partner after nine years of cohabiting but would not have considered seeing as solicitor during that time. He said:

> I didn't feel threatened. I didn't feel like I needed the advice I suppose. If we did have a problem and I thought the relationship was going pear shaped then definitely I would seek advice as to where I stood at the time when I wasn't married.

Tony and his ex-partner (and mother of his two children) had separated, but they did not want to involve solicitors in order, as he viewed it, to help keep their separation as amicable as possible:

> Well my split up is different from the average couple because we haven't got so bitter or into warfare or anything. We've always had an honest relationship—we've always been sensible enough—we're not going to cut the other person out or destroy the other person's life. There's only one person who wins then, that's the lawyers. That's where the money ends up ...

Others simply did not view the law as applicable to them. Sophie, cohabitant of two and half years with no children, when asked if she had ever thought of obtaining legal advice, replied, 'No, there's no need for that!'—the very question was somehow an attack on the strength and stability of her relationship. Similarly, Chris, cohabitant of six years and father to two young girls, did not view the law as relevant to their lives. As he put it:

> I don't know how the law stands now but I have heard that laws have changed but it wouldn't really affect us because we've no intention of splitting up anyway.

Smart and Stevens (2000) and Hibbs and colleagues (2001) also found that very few cohabitants had taken any formal legal advice. In part, this reflected a feeling that to do so would be insulting to their partner or overtly cynical about their relationship.

Not surprisingly, then, none of the interviewees had sought legal advice specifically in relation to their position as cohabitants, although particular issues did occasionally arise when they saw a solicitor in relation to a different matter. Paul, for example, had been involved in a custody battle with his ex-wife in Scotland for three years and this had made him aware of the law relating to parental responsibility. Joyce and Jack were both advised of the importance of making a will when buying a house, while Rachel found out there was a difference in the way the law treats married and unmarried fathers when she and her partner sought advice about changing her child's name:

> Yes, I didn't know there was a difference before we went … We just thought that we were living together and that if anything happened to either of us then (partner) would get it or I would get it and you give your children whatever, as long as there's somebody still there to look after your children and I just presumed that [she] would be carried on with family—I know she's not (partner's) child but she's lived as his child all her life. … I didn't realise there was any difference between being married and not being married apart from a piece of paper and a ring basically.

The media was mentioned as a primary source of information by 11 of the follow-up interviewees, although they were often vague as to the exact source. For example, Colin, cohabitant of 18 months at the time, who thought that cohabitants gain marriage-like rights after a period of 12 months living together, said that he 'read it somewhere'. Diane, who thought that legal rights were the same after five years of cohabiting, and Jane and Alex, who conversely knew that on a general level married and unmarried couples are treated differently, all mention the 'telly' or radio as their primary source of information. As we have seen, then, basing ideas on what the media supposedly relays does appear to lead to a more accurate understanding of the legal position, although it may well be that the media message is itself confused or even mistaken.

A few interviewees suggest that their legal views are influenced by information from government institutions and official forms and documentation. For example, Amanda, cohabitant of seven years who thought that cohabiting couples acquire the same rights after six months together, explains one way in which the term 'common-law husband' was introduced to her:

> Yeah. Because when … let me think … umm. When I first left me full-time job I went on that Jobseekers allowance, and (partner) was actually here, and they put him down as my common-law husband, do you know what I mean? … But say like you go for an interview, or whatever, you go in hospital and they ask you about your partner, or your relationship, blah, blah, blah, it's common-law husband, they put that down.

So in such cases the actual practice of state institutions supports or confirms misinformation and incorrect beliefs about the legal status of cohabitants. This brings us to the second question in understanding why belief in the existence of common law marriage is so widespread—just how do people evaluate information?

5 EVALUATING INFORMATION: COMMON LAW MARRIAGE AS 'LIVED LAW'

In one sense the description 'myth' is appropriate to the widespread belief in the legal existence of common law marriage, in that this belief is factually incorrect—or at least greatly exaggerated—and is maintained through informal networks that use oral traditions rather than a written code. But in other ways this appellation 'myth' is inappropriate. This is because beliefs in common law marriage, while they do not reflect the formal law, do much more closely reflect how people experience—and regulate—their everyday lives. So rather than belief in common law marriage being simply myth as fantasy, it has a real basis in material, social life. This is what we call 'lived law'[1].

A first basis for common law marriage as lived law relates to the rationale underlying people's belief in it. As we described in section 3 of this chapter, belief—or non-belief—in common law marriage rests upon notions of social logic, fairness and morality. Beliefs about what the law does are conflated with beliefs about what the law ought to do. This may help explain why the common law marriage myth is more pervasive and deeply held by people for issues where children are involved.

This moral view of what the law ought to be fits in with how people experience cohabitation in their everyday lives. Even in the legal sphere, as we have seen above, cohabitants do have some legal status and rights, even though these are usually inferior to those held by married spouses, and in the allocation of various state benefits and tax credits they are more equal. Here, government, and hence the law, treats unmarried cohabitants as husband and wife in applying eligibility rules about joint income and expenditures. As a result, state bodies have come up with various definitions of cohabitation, most based upon evidence of shared living arrangements, a sexual relationship, stability, financial support, the presence of children and public acknowledgement (Davies, 1999). These definitions are then used to equate such couples with married couples. For example the Inland Revenue's 2004 Child Tax Credit application form helpfully includes those who 'live with someone as if you are married … as a couple' along with the formally married. Other institutions, such as insurance and utility companies, can also use

---

[1] The notion of 'lived law' has been developed in Development Studies in researching social practices in sub-Saharan Africa. In this context everyday village life is partly regulated through informal social custom and practice, drawing on but not hidebound by historically developed traditions. This 'lived law' is sometimes contradictory to the formal law of colonial and post colonial states. See for example, Hodgson, 2000; Odgard, 2002.

common law marriage as a definitional category. Their treatment of customers, for example in working out premiums, may differ as a result (one of the authors regularly embarrasses himself in trying to explain—unsuccessfully—to call centre workers that this category does not exist). Such official definitions can promote a quite powerful validation of the 'myth', because many people will have day-to-day experience of this parity. Again, this is an area where periodic experience will validate the 'myth'.

Even more powerfully, the idea of common law marriage is validated by day-to-day practice in everyday life. Thus, as we saw in chapter 2, heterosexual cohabitants, certainly those with children and/or some length of co-residence, are commonly treated as 'man and wife'. Socially, they are usually treated as an exclusive couple, and the female partner is often referred to as 'Mrs'. Similarly the cohabitants themselves will often present themselves in an equivalent way, even at times referring to their 'in-laws'. In maternity wards, doctor's surgeries, school meetings, work parties and social gatherings throughout the land cohabitants will receive affirmation of married status. Or, increasingly, married spouses will be treated as cohabitants by inclusion in the more universal category of 'partner'. For all these reasons the common law marriage myth is perhaps best understood as a variety of 'lived law'. In turn this 'lived law' receives further validation in that cohabitation is now so widely practised and accepted across Britain (see chapter 2).

6 CONCLUSION: BELIEFS, MORALITIES AND CONCERNS

In 2000, a majority of the British public believed that married and unmarried couples have the same legal rights and responsibilities, and this belief was pervasive among all social groups and geographical areas. The in-depth study showed a layering in this belief, however. For the 'believers' time eligibility varied; some believed common law marriage is triggered on the day a couple move in together and others believed this occurred after a period of time, ranging from six months to six years. This notion of time eligibility spilt over into ideas about income and property rights, such as maintenance and inheritance. However, rights and duties concerning children were seen as less time based. A further layer of belief related to specific legal issues and here belief in the legal effects of common law marriage contracts and expands. For issues where children are involved, the common law marriage myth is more pervasive and deeply held, while for property issues belief in the legal status common law marriage is somewhat less widespread, and—where believed—is seen as less favourable to cohabitants. This layering is not surprising and people tend to assume that the law will reflect what they see as socially logical and morally sensible.

Generally, the interviews point to an informal knowledge world where most respondents get the bulk of their information from friends and family. There is no uniformity of belief as to what the law 'does' in relation to cohabitants reflecting the influence of context on people's assumptions as to the purpose and nature of legal frameworks. In this sense the description 'myth' is appropriate to the widespread belief in the legal existence of common law marriage, in that this belief is factually incorrect—or at least greatly exaggerated—and is maintained through informal networks that use oral traditions rather than a written code. But in other ways this appellation 'myth' is inappropriate and is perhaps best understood as a variety of 'lived law'.

This disjuncture between the 'lived law' of common law marriage and formal law causes concern as an increasing number of people in 21st century Britain will cohabit outside marriage at some point in their lives, and many of these will have children (see chapter 2). Few of these cohabitants will be aware that the formal law does not protect them and their families in the way that it protects married couples. Is this disjuncture between lived law and 'real', formal law the reason why people in Britain are increasingly cohabiting outside marriage, despite all the legal disadvantages to doing so? The next chapter goes on to deal with the question—just why do people cohabit instead of marrying?

4

Why Cohabit? Commitment and Alternative Rationalities

1 INTRODUCTION: UNMARRIED COHABITATION AS IRRATIONAL BEHAVIOUR?

Chapter 2 has shown that unmarried heterosexual cohabitation is both widely practised and accepted in Britain. The BSA survey showed that in 2000 over a third of people under 35 who lived with a partner were unmarried, and over 80 per cent of this age group viewed cohabitation without marriage as 'all right'. By 2004, over a quarter of births were to unmarried cohabitants, and in 2000 around 60 per cent of this age group also thought this acceptable. Nor, as far as we can tell, is this a life course effect, when attitudes change as people get older (the result of jointly acquiring children or property perhaps). Rather this is a generational effect where attitudes are relatively unaffected by this ageing process, although it does appear that all age groups are becoming more accepting over time. Even so, while older people practice cohabitation less, the majority are still accepting of it—and even think it is a good idea before marriage—while cohabitation is common for older people in particular circumstances, for example with a new partner after divorce. Similarly, there was little difference by social class, except that it is more likely for the better off to get married when they have children. Consequently, both the incidence of cohabitation, and the numbers of children with unmarried, but cohabiting parents, are expected to increase substantially over coming decades. In this way Britain seems to be moving towards a Scandinavian pattern, where unmarried cohabitation is quite normal and where marriage is more of a lifestyle choice rather than an expected part of life.

At first sight all this seems like mass irrationality. For, as chapter 1 discussed in detail, marriage gives partners substantial and automatic legal benefits which they do not possess as unmarried cohabitants. In brief, married spouses automatically acquire rights to reasonable financial support from their partner, occupation rights in the matrimonial home, exemption from capital gains and inheritance tax for asset transfers between each other, access to financial support on divorce or separation, automatic joint parental responsibility, better protection from domestic violence, succession into a partner's pension and automatic entitlement into their estate on death if no will has been made. It is not that cohabitants do not have any legal rights. In some situations the law even treats cohabitants as equal to married spouses—notably in allocating means tested benefits or tax credits (although even then the partner in receipt has no legal duty to share this income!). In other situations, the law does recognise the familial nature of cohabitation to some extent, but sees this as inferior to marriage (for example in Inheritance Act claims on a deceased partner's estate). In yet other circumstances, the law simply treats cohabitants—even long standing ones with children—as complete strangers (as with pension payments and partner maintenance). For cohabitants the law is confusing, complex, usually inferior, and hardly ever automatic. Those people—generally children and caring dependants—who are the most vulnerable in families, especially on breakdown or death, are particularly vulnerable as cohabiting family members.

There are legal remedies to which cohabitants can turn in tackling some of these disadvantages. For example, they can take out written agreements about shares in the ownership of the family home, they can make or change a will to secure inheritance for their partner, and fathers can make parental responsibility agreements with the mother or apply for a parental responsibility order (before 1 December 2003 mothers otherwise automatically retained sole parental rights, although since then fathers who jointly register the childbirth also receive parental rights). Yet the 2000 BSA survey showed that very few had made these safeguards, only 14 per cent of then current cohabitants had changed or made wills, just nine per cent had made property agreements, and an even lower proportion of fathers—just five per cent—had obtained parental responsibility agreements or orders. Most cohabitants remained in a vulnerable legal situation.

It could be the case that a simple gender division explains this apparent irrationality. For legal vulnerability in a relationship will be double-edged. That is, the more powerful or secure cohabitant may gain as the weaker lose out. Male partners are often the least dependent, at least in financial terms; they usually have the higher paying, more secure job with pension rights and are most likely to be the house owner. They could act in a rationally selfish way to gain all the benefits of a relationship with a female partner without the legal disadvantages if things went wrong; they could even remedy the major defect in this strategy—the lack of a legal relationship with any children—by making a parental responsibility agreement/order (and since 1 December 2003 this has become automatic with joint registration of the birth). However, quite apart from all the evidence that suggests male partners do not usually think in this way (see below), they have clearly not followed this strategy very well, when so few had in fact taken out parental agreements/orders. Furthermore, while women are the ones who in the main would be the most vulnerable, there is in fact little gender difference in attitudes towards cohabitation. Indeed, as chapter 2 shows, if anything women—especially younger women—are more ambivalent about marriage, and more in favour of cohabitation.

Nor can we suppose that marriage is too expensive or difficult to arrange. Not only is cohabitation common in all income groups, but in 2004 an expenditure of only £94—for a register office marriage—would secure all the legal benefits on offer. Even with associated extra costs—the hire of a suit, a new dress, a cake, sandwiches for a few friends (to apply the practice of many marriages in the 1950s and 60s)—this is quite a bargain. All this takes is a simple application and booking a date. Unlike some European countries, pre-nuptial legal arrangements are not necessary, and despite often being called a 'marriage contract', legal provisions on marriage are automatic and standard. As His Honour Judge Hannen put it in a landmark ruling in 1885, with the whiff of arrogance that sometimes permeates legal pronouncements:

> The contract of marriage is a simple one, which does not require a high degree of intellect to comprehend[1].

Cohabitation rights such as they are, in contrast, require some legal ability to fully comprehend and even many family lawyers admit to being confused.

Now the evidence shows that most spouses-to-be want more than this simple register office ceremony and the 'average wedding' in 2002 cost nearly £12,000. The typical reception alone cost over £4,000, with rings at £1,500. Even the photographer cost over £500 (Wedding and Home Magazine, *The Guardian* 11 May 2002). By 2004 one source estimated as much as £17,740 (The Wedding Agenda, May/June 2004). As a result of this high, and it seems increasing, cost of the desired wedding many take out insurance to cover ruined clothes, bankrupt caterers, and the like. Planning and preparation can take a year or more. So why do cohabitants not simply secure their legal position as cohabitants by consulting a lawyer and carrying out a few standard legal procedures, all for much less than £12,000? Or why do they not simply get married, cheaply and easily for a few hundred pounds, and gain the substantial legal benefits and security available to them?

There are two possible answers to these questions. One is legal ignorance, or at least misinformation and lack of knowledge. As discussed in chapter 3, the BSA survey shows that in 2000 over half of all cohabitants believed, incorrectly, in 'common-law marriage' whereby they would supposedly gain marriage-like rights through cohabitation. Another explanation is that cohabitants act according to different rationalities than the instrumental legal rationality we have described so far. Either there is a different set of costs and benefits to those we have outlined, which override the legal costs of cohabiting instead of marrying, or people do not act in this simple individualistic cost-benefit way at all, but

---

[1] *Durham v Durham* (1885) 10 PD 80, 82. Taken from Hibbs *et al*, 2001.

instead consider a wider set of social, moral and emotional factors in making the decision to marry or not. We will now turn to these explanations, which are not mutually exclusive, in the following sections.

2 EXPLAINING IRRATIONALITY? LACK OF KNOWLEDGE AND THE COMMON LAW MARRIAGE MYTH

In 2002 the Law Commission reported on its investigation into the property rights of cohabitants and other 'home-sharers' in the family home (Law Commission, 2002). Fully acknowledging that the legal problems that cohabitants experience, as outlined above, were 'unfair, uncertain and illogical' the Commission nonetheless found it impossible to recommend a better legal approach. This has been called an 'extraordinary failure' (Dyer, 2002) and it is one of the aims of this book to show that legal reforms are, in fact, possible (see chapters 5 and 6). Yet the residual recommendations made by the Law Commission in lieu are indicative for our purposes here. For, having abandoned reform—and by implication the view that cohabitants were in some way acting reasonably and so deserved a legal response—the Law Commission was forced to see cohabitants as either simply ignorant of the law or, at the other extreme, potential legal buffs with a cost-benefit agenda. On the one hand unmarried cohabitants should draw up a declaration of trust for the determination of shares in their home (as we have seen, this seems unlikely). At the other extreme, as Stuart Bridge, the Law Commissioner for property and trust law, put it:

> We must emphasise that there is no such thing as common law marriage in England and Wales. If people think they obtain rights by living together for a period of time they are wrong. They must be disabused of that (*The Guardian*, 19 July 2002).

Partly in response to this recommendation, and to the BSA 2000 evidence that a majority of people do indeed believe in some sort of 'common law marriage', the government has undertaken a publicity programme to this effect, led by the Department for Constitutional Affairs (*The Guardian*, 18 November 2003).

At first sight the 'common law marriage myth' does give a plausible explanation of cohabitants' apparent irrationality in not getting married. For, as chapter 3 showed, this 'myth' is widely believed. If marriage-like rights come automatically after a certain period of cohabitation, and/or after joint registration of a child—as many believe—then there is clearly much less need to go to the expense, practical trouble and possible emotional confrontation with oneself and others of getting married. So Diane, who had been cohabiting for just a year, and had one child, simply thought:

Well, what's the point of getting married because we're classed as though we're married—we're living together and if we do split up we still do what a married couple would do—split everything, kids, responsibility and everything.

However, as soon as we examine this 'lack of knowledge' explanation further, we find that at best it can only provide a partial and superficial explanation of the rising tide of unmarried cohabitation.

A first problem for this explanation simply lies in the historical trends. For, while unmarried cohabitation is rapidly increasing, it seems reasonable to assume that belief in common law marriage is decreasing. According to the 2000 BSA survey, 56 per cent of people in Britain then thought that unmarried couples who lived together for some time 'definitely' or 'probably' had a common law marriage, compared to just 37 per cent who correctly believed they did not (see chapter 3). As this survey provides the first representative quantitative measure of the common law marriage myth, we cannot be sure of historical trends, but what evidence that can be pieced together suggests that although belief in common law marriage was widespread in the nineteenth and twentieth centuries (see Kiernan and Estaugh, 1993), it had been gradually decreasing since its actual legal abolition in 1753. Lawrence Stone, in his magisterial book on the Road to Divorce in England (1990) describes how the 1753 law banning common law marriage:

> flew directly in the face of a rising tide of demand, fuelled partly by individualism and romanticism, but above all by a dogged desire for privacy, itself a product of the traditional freedom of pre-marital social relations and sexual experimentation among the English poor (135–6).

Consequently, both the accounts of contemporaries and available evidence (such as the bastardy rates) suggest large scale unmarried cohabitation in the late eighteenth century. According to David Johnson, following the 1753 Marriage Act,

> the poor, without any significant concerns about property and inheritance, and therefore no need for recourse to law, could simply ignore the legislation altogether (2003:43).

Certainly non-marital parenthood often attained the social status of legal marriage, and this continued during the Victorian period especially in poorer neighbourhoods (Laslett et al, 1980; Gillis, 1985). However, the historical evidence suggests unmarried cohabitation was decreasing throughout the nineteenth century, as the 1753 Act became part of a more general, moral shift towards 'Victorian' family values. Indeed, by the time Queen Victoria came to the throne in 1837 the earlier rise in illegitimacy had been reversed as pregnancies outside marriage fell from around 40 per cent to 20 per cent (Johnson, 2003). Nonetheless, this is still a substantial minority and by the early twentieth century, Charles Booth noted that unmarried cohabitation was common among the labouring population in London, and in the First World War the government was forced to extend Separation Allowances to 'common law wives' of servicemen when the extent of this relationship was realised (despite objections from religious authorities). Colloquial terms for common law marriage, such as 'living tally' in Wales and 'living over t'brush' in northern England seem to have been in general usage in some places even after the Second World War (Kiernan and Estaugh, 1993). What the historical evidence points towards is the gradually decreasing practice of unmarried cohabitation from the late eighteenth up to the mid twentieth century, and a concomitant decrease in belief in the legal existence of common law marriage. While we have no direct evidence, the spread of education, the deeper influence of mass media, and an increasing 'legalisation' of society (for example as people are more likely to consult lawyers in buying homes and other property, in getting divorced and so on) would surely reduce belief in common law marriage. The alternative— to assume that people are becoming less legally aware over time, that this ignorance of the law is increasingly spreading among the well-educated and rich just as much as the ill-educated and poor, and hence belief in common law marriage is galloping apace—is somewhat counter-intuitive.

A second major problem with the 'lack of knowledge' explanation lies in the very longevity and enormity of this myth. For Common Law Marriage, which did at one time legally exist, was abolished by Act of Parliament in 1753 (see chapter 3). How is it that such completely incorrect legal assumptions survive (or have been resurrected) more than 250 years later, a quarter of a millennium, for over half the British population? In contrast, by 2000 nearly everyone knew that homosexual relations for male adults were no longer illegal—a mere 33 years since the Sexual Offences Act in 1967. Similarly most people know that simple breakdown of a marriage with separation is sufficient grounds for divorce; complicated and embarrassing legal proof of fault is no longer required since the liberalisation of divorce law with the 1969 Divorce Reform Act. It is not the case that ordinary members of the public are experts on laws about sexual behaviour or divorce law, rather they are aware of the general direction and message; certainly they are not so spectacularly and pervasively wrong as with common law marriage. We might perhaps expect that those who had not been cohabiting very long, or who were ill-educated, might show less knowledge—but both the national BSA survey and the in-depth interviews found that belief in the common law myth was common among all ages, social classes, and educational levels, and for single people, unmarried cohabitants (both short and long term) and married spouses alike (see chapter 3). Both the longevity and pervasiveness of the common law marriage myth, and the enormous gulf between myth and law, point to another explanation; the idea of common law marriage chimes in with people's everyday 'lived' experience in some way. This returns us to common law marriage as 'lived law', as described in chapter 3. Unmarried cohabitants, especially those living together some time and/or with children, are usually treated as if they were married by state institutions, commercial firms, and everyday contacts in workplaces, communities and neighbourhoods.

A third problem with the 'lack of knowledge' explanation for the prevalence of cohabitation, using the common law marriage myth as prop, is the behaviour of the third of the British population in 2000 who did *not* believe that common law marriage exists, in the sense of cohabitation giving marriage-like legal rights. For there is little evidence of any increase in legal rationality in this group, compared to those who did believe the 'myth'. Indeed, there was no difference at all in the BSA 2000 survey between cohabitants in this non-believing group, and cohabiting 'myth believers', in the proportions who had taken out parental responsibility agreements/orders or who had made property agreements. While 15 per cent of the non-believing group had made or changed a will as a result of cohabiting, nine per cent of the 'myth believers' had done so; this is hardly a profound difference.

This lack of legal rationality was equally evident in our follow-up interviews. In most cases people's perceptions of the legal consequences, whether accurate or inaccurate, had no impact on their decision to cohabit or marry. For example, Melanie had been living with her partner and her two sons from a previous relationship for ten years at the time of interview and thought that married and unmarried couples have similar legal rights. When asked if her (albeit inaccurate) knowledge of the legal situation had an impact on her decision to cohabit she said:

> I don't think that affects us—or my choice or what I'm doing in any way.

Similarly, Jessica, cohabiting for 12 years and with two daughters, expressed surprise at this question:

> Not at all, that never crossed our minds.

There were a few exceptions, where respondents had some knowledge of the correct legal situation and intended to do something about it, but even then nothing much had actually happened. Lynda gives a stark example, because although cohabiting for eight and a half years, with two children, she was in fact still married to someone else! This was because the legal situation was just 'fine-tuning' something that, in her view, was already sorted. As she explained:

> I did get a couple of forms and did actually make an appointment with a solicitor to sort of fine tune but it's something unfortunately that you tend to put off—again for financial reasons like paying the solicitor and I want to find out as much information myself. The more I can find out the less legal advice I will need and also the more choice I can make for myself.

This lack of legal rationality is equally apparent for those who do marry. Thus Mary Hibbs and colleagues found that 41 per cent of their 1998/99 sample of 173

engaged respondents (three quarters of whom were cohabiting) thought that marriage would not change the legal nature of their relationship. As many as 37 per
cent even saw no legal consequences of marriage for present or future children.
Indeed, Hibbs and colleagues found only one respondent who cited 'legal reasons'
as a cause for marriage, and only three per cent of their respondents admitted to
any legal influence at all. Similarly, in 2002 John Eekelaar and Mavis Maclean
(2004) found only one out of 39 respondents who admitted to legal considerations
as a reason for marrying. Most of our respondents, like those interviewed by Hibbs
and colleagues, were likely to view questions about legal measures with surprise
or even indignation. What had marriage and living together to do with the law?—
And in any case they trusted and loved their partners. There was no need for a formal public document making their wish to have a union explicit, and it was the private promises between the partners that were regarded as the important thing. Nor
is this just a specific British consensus: much the same can be described in many
other European countries (for example Björnberg 2001 for Sweden). This supports
the views of comparative demographers that increasing cohabitation is part of a
widespread change in expectations about intimacy and partnership in modern societies, rather than the product of particular national legal situations (see Lesthaeghe
1995; Prinz, 1995; Gonzalez-Lopez and Solsona, 2000). Duncan, a schoolteacher
who had been cohabiting for 5 years, gives a nice summary of this consensus:

> ... there are some things that you are better off if you are married but then
> that's not the final reason for getting married, what's the point of getting
> married if it's just to save money on your income tax or your pensions or
> whatever else it might be ... They're not good reasons in my view ...

This response perhaps indicates the key to why people cohabit rather than marry;
they see living together as an emotional relationship, not an economic transaction.
This is in some contrast to the context in which common law marriage was abolished over 250 years ago: a prime concern of the Clandestine Marriages Act in
1753 was indeed to protect aristocratic property rights (Johnson, 2003).

In the next sections we will examine how people in Britain today view partnering arrangements, as opposed to how the law sees them, and how this can
make unmarried cohabitation seem the sensible, rational option. We will start by
asking whether cohabiting partners have low levels of commitment to their partnerships. If they lack commitment then marriage—which despite high divorce
rates does involve formal and public commitment to the longer term—would
indeed not be an attractive or indeed rational option.

3 COHABITATION AND COMMITMENT

In the political and media discourse commitment to a relationship is usually
equated with marriage. Partners who are committed to one another get married,

unless—and this is a more recent addition to the argument—they are misled by the common law marriage myth. In this discourse, cohabitation is viewed as a second-rate family structure, characterised as fragile (eg Ermisch, 2002; Ermisch and Franscesconi, 1999; Haskey, 1999 and 2001), informal (eg Schoen and Weinick, 1993), an 'incomplete institution' (Nock, 1995) and 'lacking commitment' (P Morgan, 1999). This assumption is supported by reference to statistical comparisons, where on average married spouses are less likely to break up, and when marriages last for longer than cohabiting relationships. Marriage is seen as the ideal to which all couples aspire, or should do. This is why the 1998 Green Paper *Supporting Families* devoted a whole chapter to 'Strengthening marriage', with only cursory reference to unmarried cohabitation (Home Office, 1998; see Barlow and Duncan, 2000). The legal reflection of this assumption is illustrated by the Family Law Act 1996. Cohabitation is defined as an arrangement where:

> a man and a woman who, although not married to each other, are living together as husband and wife (s62(1)) where judges should have regard to the fact that [the cohabitants] have not given each other the commitment involved in marriage (s41).

This is a picture that many cohabitants would not recognise, still less agree with. Empirical studies, including our own, routinely record expressions of commitment by cohabitants that are little different from those of married spouses (see also C Lewis et al, 2002; J Lewis, 2001; Eekelaar and Maclean, 2004). As Charlie Lewis and colleagues point out, 'The word used by the vast majority of interviewees to describe cohabitation was 'commitment' (2002: 10). In our survey, for example, Nigel—a retired head teacher with one stepdaughter—felt that:

> my commitment to the relationship and our family is absolute

while Susan favourably compared her current cohabiting union to a previous marriage:

> I don't see it as being married or not. What I do is compare my relationship, my and Mike's relationship, with the person I was with before regardless of the fact that I was married to one and not to the other, and it's how happy I am and how the relationship's working, and I think that's much more important than the fact that one was a marriage and one isn't.

The implication that marriage was in some way better evoked some heated responses from respondents. Natasha, talking about parenting (she had three children over a 12 year partnership), responded:

> Why should kids be any happier if your parents are married or whether they're not married. I can't honestly see there being any difference. That

> married couple's kids may have Reebok trainers—so have my kids. Their
> kids know right from wrong, so do my kids … You cannot tell me that there
> is any child, whether you are married or unmarried, that doesn't do anything
> wrong—doesn't swear, doesn't smoke behind your back—in all honesty
> there's no difference.

Amanda, cohabiting for two years, was particularly scathing about the assumed
advantages of marriage:

> It's like they're wearing rose-coloured glasses because I know a lot of peo-
> ple that are married and they're rowing, they're screaming, the kids live,
> uum, in a horrible atmosphere.

Indeed some cohabitants claimed that the lack of a formal, legal union demands
greater commitment on their part, and more attention to their partner and the relationship. This means cohabitation is the more ethically sound and honest relationship (see also C Lewis, 2002). For Melanie, who had also been married
before:

> At least this way you know you're together because you love each other and
> you want to be together.

As Jane Lewis (2001) reflects from her sample, in this way it is unmarried cohabitants, not married spouses, who can claim the moral high ground.

The statistical evidence brought to support the 'marriage equals commitment'
assumption seems compelling at first sight, in that it reflects what people actually do rather than what they say. The fact that cohabitants are more likely to break
up, and their unions last for less time, appears to speak more about commitment
than their happiness, aspirations or expectations, however sincerely expressed.
However, this evidence is largely tautological; it commits the statistical error of
not comparing like with like. First and foremost, the married population is on
average older than the cohabiting population; only around 20 per cent of the married population is under 35, and just two per cent under 25, compared to nearly
70 per cent and 20 per cent, respectively, of cohabitants. The age at which partnership starts is one of the most powerful factors associated with subsequent
breakdown: younger unions—whether married or not—are less stable in both
emotional and structural terms (Murphy, 1985; Gibson, 2000). Quite apart from
personality and emotional issues, income, jobs and housing will be less secure
and fixed (Haskey, 1983; Thornes and Collard, 1979). If the cohabiting and married populations had the same age structures this factor alone would substantially reduce differences in breakdown rates.

Secondly, cohabiting couples are less likely to have children, partly because of
their younger age, and the presence of a child has been estimated to reduce breakdown rates by as much as 40 per cent (Haskey, 1983; Murphy, 1985). Research

also shows that there is very little difference in 'relationship quality' between cohabitants and married spouses who had children, or who wanted children (Brown and Booth, 1996). Third, the cohabiting population includes those who are living together before marriage, often explicitly seen as a 'trial marriage' where a long-term commitment has not yet been made. By the early 1990s 70 per cent of marriages were preceded by cohabitation, as opposed to just ten per cent in the early 1970s (Haskey, 2001). In this way cohabitation has increasingly replaced unmarried engagement, where partners did not live together but where sexual relations were often socially accepted in the run-up to a wedding. And as cohabitation becomes a longer-term replacement for marriage, 'trial marriage' will be increasingly replaced by what we might call 'trial cohabitation'. That is, cohabitation may at first be experienced as a test of living together—unmarried— over the longer term. Fourth, cohabitation often follows marriage breakdown; this 'post-separation cohabitation' has increasingly replaced remarriage, where the remarried were at a much higher risk of breakdown. Finally, the married popula- tion includes partners who find it difficult to separate because of external pres- sures, like those of religion or family pressure. If we compared like with like, for example young childless couples, or older couples in a long-term union with chil- dren, there would probably be little difference between separation rates for cohabiting and married couples.

This is certainly what the evidence suggests. Thus 23 per cent of the BSA 2000 sample of cohabitants had been together for over ten years. It is not possible or meaningful (just because so many marriages date from a time when cohabitation was uncommon) to give an average length of marriage, but the median duration of those 40 per cent of marriages currently ending in divorce is also around ten years. And the younger the age of partners at marriage, the higher the rates of breakdown (Haskey, 1983). The example of the 'shotgun marriage'—where partners were vir- tually forced to marry after an unplanned pregnancy—is particularly telling. This social institution of the 1950s and 60s is now virtually extinct, and in 2000 only three per cent of marriages were preceded by pre-marital conceptions, compared to almost a quarter in 1970. Shotgun marriages were notorious for high rates of dysfunctionality and breakdown (Thornes and Collard, 1979); one study of the 1960s found that 41 per cent of marriages with a pre-marital pregnancy had dis- solved after only 5 years, compared with 18 per cent of those who had not con- ceived pre-maritally (Coombs and Zumeta, 1970). Shotgun marriages seem to have been replaced by—less forced—unmarried cohabitation. These particular cohabiting partnerships will often be among the less committed: indeed unplanned pregnancy was a common feature of what Carol Smart and Pippa Stevens (2000) have called the 'contingent commitment' expressed by some former, separated cohabitants. Rachel, cohabiting for three years, expressed it like this:

> We were just sort of going out with each other and it was nothing serious,
> well obviously it was serious because I then found out I was pregnant with

(daughter) and we then just steadily went on—I was living with (son) on my own and it just seemed a good idea for (partner) and he just decided we should buy somewhere together and all live together and it just came about—it was a shotgun thing.

Unexpected cohabitation like this will probably still have the better track record compared to shotgun marriages however; it demands some level of personal rather than forced commitment and escapes the pressures resulting from ideal expectations surrounding marriage. As Natasha Walter has put it, 'If you don't already have it, you aren't going to get it from the vicar and the cake' (*The Guardian*, 28 November 2003).

If we are to compare commitment between married and unmarried cohabiting partners, we need to define what it is and what makes it up. After a wide-ranging discussion of various attempts to do this, Jane Lewis (2001) comes back to Johnson's (1991) distinction of three dimensions to commitment. These are:

1   Personal commitment to the partner, summed up as wanting the relationship to continue.
2   Moral-normative commitment, summed up as the feeling that the relationship ought to continue.
3   Structural commitment, summed up as the feeling that a relationship has to continue because of the investments made in the relationship (eg housing, finance, job arrangements, children), and costs of ending it.

As we have discussed above, many, if not most, cohabitants display the first, more personal, dimension to commitment. There may be some types of cohabitation where partners do not feel this commitment so completely, such as the more 'contingently committed' unions following an unexpected pregnancy. Equally, there will be marriages where this dimension is weak. Arranged marriages, 'shotgun' marriages, or those made for largely economic reasons, can be examples. In these cases it will be dimensions 2 and 3 that keep the partnership intact. While structural commitment, dimension 3, is not normally felt or experienced until dimensions 1 and 2 are weak and the partnership is liable to break up, it is easy to show that most cohabitants will be as subject to these constraints as married spouses. For studies show that divisions of labour, leisure behaviour, the sharing of property and income, and joint responsibility for children are virtually identical for married and cohabiting couples (C Lewis et al, 2002; J Lewis, 2001; Eekelaar and Maclean, 2004). Virtually identical, that is, if age is taken into account, for practices seem to vary much more by generation than by the form of the union. Again, there are some exceptions. For example, younger cohabitants undertaking a trial marriage will often share a house rental, rather than the more constraining mortgaged ownership (indeed getting a mortgage often signals long-term commitment).

Our own interviews confirmed this general consensus. As Sharon, cohabiting for seven years and with three children, put it:

> If you're living together, you've still got bills together.

We found a continuum in the management of household finances; some cohabitants held separate accounts and paid their way as individuals as if just sharing a house rather than living together as a couple, others pooled all income and jointly managed finances. While there was some polarisation, the majority of the 48 respondents managed finances jointly. This is rather like the pattern for married couples (Laurie and Gershuny, 2000). Although separate management itself does not necessarily mean lack of commitment, it was those former cohabitants who had subsequently separated, and who in turn were mostly younger people involved in trial marriage, who were most likely to hold separate financial arrangements. Involvement in household chores and childcare showed a similar distribution, and again this was very much like that for married couples where the divide was between men and women, not between cohabiting and married partners. Indeed, if lack of joint involvement in childcare and household chores is taken as an index of commitment to a relationship, then some married couples must be very uncommitted indeed!

We might expect that cohabitants would differ more from married couples on the second dimension of commitment identified above: moral-normative views that the relationship ought to continue. There is some evidence that this can be the case. For a small sample of separated cohabitants with children, Charlie Lewis and colleagues (2002) found that some respondents saw cohabitation as offering greater freedom to monitor, re-evaluate and negotiate their relationships at any time. And if people 'grew apart', relationships could more easily be ended. In comparison, these same respondents thought of marriage as putting people under pressure to stay together despite such changes—sometimes seen negatively in terms of preventing self-development and honesty, but sometimes seen as a positive feature just because of the feeling that important relationships 'ought to continue'. In contrast Jane Lewis (2001), using another small sample but this time of long-established partnerships with children, found that the association between obligation and marriage was restricted to an older generation married in the 50s and 60s. Their own children aged between 27 and 50, whether married or cohabiting, all believed that commitment came from within—from love of the other person and their children—rather than any externally prescribed moral code. The only difference between cohabitants and married spouses for this group concerned the wider presentation of their commitment. Cohabitants saw their commitment as private whereas those who had married (often after long-term cohabitation) felt the need to make a public commitment. For the cohabitants, commitment was private in two senses— it was theirs alone and did not involve state, church, community or kin, and it eschewed any public ceremony. For the married couples, public commitment seemed to be most important for relatives and kin, especially the parents, who then knew where the relationship stood and how they should behave as a result. This is seemingly echoed by Eekelaar and Maclean's (2004) discovery that marriage was often undertaken as a matter of 'conformity', and was particularly aimed at pleasing relatives. But the more private commitment made by cohabitants does not necessarily mean it is a weaker or lesser commitment. Indeed all the Jane Lewis sample acknowledged the importance of the fact that they had made a commitment. Our own interviews of cohabitants came up with a similar response: marriage was basically about making commitment public—sometimes seen negatively as just showing off or keeping up with the Joneses. But the basis for their partnership was a strong private commitment to another person.

We can bring together, and summarise, these various dimensions of commitment by adapting the notions of 'mutual' and 'contingent' commitment, first developed by Carol Smart and Pippa Stevens (2000). Table 4.1 below adapts this model.

TABLE 4.1 *Mutual and contingent commitment*

Contingent commitment ←——— continuum ———→ **mutual commitment**	
— the couple have not known each other for long	— the relationship is established before cohabiting
— legal and financial agreements are absent	— there are some legal and financial agreements
— children are not planned (although they may be wanted)	— children are planned and wanted by both parents
— pregnancy predates the cohabitation	— pregnancy postdates cohabitation, and both parents are involved in childcare
— significant personal change is needed for	— there are mutually agreed expectations of the relationship
— there is no presumption that the relationship will last—only a hope	— there is a presumption that the relationship will last

Source: adapted from Smart and Stevens, 2000.

This model contrasts two ideal, polarised types of commitment, and Smart and Stevens are at pains to point out that most couples will be located on the continuum between the two poles. Similarly, partnerships are not static but will move along this range. Not surprisingly, given that Smart and Stevens were examining cohabitation breakdown, a majority of their respondents were located toward the contingent side of the spectrum. We might expect that the long-established, apparently successful and committed partnerships examined by Jane Lewis (2001), discussed above, would be located on the mutual side. The interviews from our own in depth study give a better basis than these specific, purposive samples for summarising this material about cohabitation and commitment, in that they were taken from the BSA survey of British households. While not representative in population terms, these interviews do cover a wide range of types of cohabitation—long-established and short-term, pre-marriage and alternative to marriage, with and without children, older and younger partners, and so on (see Appendix 1). We located each of the 48 interviewees along the contingent-mutual commitment continuum by reference to both their expressed understandings and feelings about their partnership, their motivations for living together, and their behaviour within the partnership (in gender divisions of labour, in sharing finances, in drawing up legal arrangements). As Figure 4.1 shows, the majority of the follow-up interviewees, taken from a range of cohabitation experiences and types, were located towards the mutual committed end of the continuum. While some cohabitants will show less commitment than this, the evidence does simply not support the 'official' assumption that cohabitation means contingent commitment. It would appear that most cohabitants are as committed to one another, and to the relationship, as married couples are supposed to be.

FIGURE 4.1 *Cohabitation and commitment: follow-up interviewees*

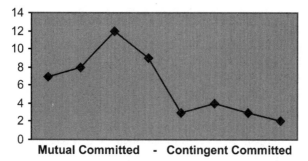

Source: interviews, 2001.

So far we have mainly looked at commitment within cohabiting partnerships. We should also remember that marriage itself has changed substantially over recent decades. It has slowly left its patriarchal origins in both law and social practice—Stone describes the legal position of wives in England right up to the early nineteenth century as 'the nearest approximation in a free society to a slave' (1990: 13)—and is emerging as more of an equal partnership. Despite often unequal gender divisions of labour and a continuing polarisation of male and female identities around providing and caring, marriage has become more companionate where spouses see themselves as emotional and social equals. Partly as a result of this, in that expectations are less easily realised and can more easily change, marriage is no longer necessarily a lifelong commitment. Certainly it is widely no longer seen as such (J Lewis, 2001). Similarly, marriage does not necessarily mean high levels of commitment; among Eekelaar and Maclean's (2004) sample of 24 married couples for example, several had low expectations of their partnership, and hence low levels of commitment to it. It is this change, rather than the liberalisation in divorce laws, that is associated with increasing rates of divorce. After all, you have to want to divorce to use the more liberal legislation, or, as Christopher Prinz puts it:

> Today, divorce is a functional necessity in view of the social changes; it is a safeguard without which living together would become a practical impossibility or at best extremely risky (1995, 86).

This is why many of the divorcees interviewed by Smart and colleagues in a series of studies (Smart, 2004) no longer saw divorce as personal tragedy, a view held by the interviewees' elderly parents (mostly still married). Rather, divorce has become 'normalised', a widespread social phenomenon that is part of the life course, almost 'a kind of modern rite of passage,' which is associated with personal growth and maturity (Smart, 2004). And just as there are different reasons for cohabiting, so there are different reasons for marrying. This includes commitment to the other partner and the relationship, but not exclusively so; marriage has often been something of a 'career move' for many women, and 'conformity', obligations to parents and kin, religious mores, migration and economic motives can all play a part in the decision to marry.

In this section we have seen that many unmarried cohabitants see themselves as being just as committed to their partners as married people and—if we compare like with like—that their behaviour seems to bear this out. As Jane Lewis (2001) concluded, the crucial thing for the majority is the existence of commitment, rather than whether it is manifested as marriage or unmarried cohabitation. While there are different types of cohabitation and marriage, and both may show a range of commitment, it is certainly not the case that cohabitation necessarily reflects, or causes, weaker or lower levels of commitment. This means, in turn, that by and large cohabiting partners do not avoid marriage because of low levels of commitment.

This conclusion returns us to our original problem, however. If cohabiting partners are mostly just as committed as married spouses, and if many can gain substantial legal benefits, and potential economic gains, from marriage, then why do they not do so? In fact the problem is compounded, for rather than seeing partners as selfish individuals (where the economically stronger might rationally avoid marriage), we can now see them as committed and caring individuals who presumably would like their partners and children to have the full protection of the law. Certainly, as chapter 5 will go on to show in detail, a large majority thinks that the legal benefits of marriage should be extended to cohabitants.

So far in this chapter we have shown that cohabitants' behaviour is explained by neither (a) a mass lack of knowledge about their legal inferiority to married couples (the 'follow-up' assumption being that this can therefore be remedied by correct information), or (b) a lack of commitment to each other (the 'follow-up' assumption here being that they do not want or deserve the legal protection given to supposedly more committed married couples). These findings are important when considering the options for legal reform (see chapters 5 and 6). However, if we do rule out lack of knowledge or commitment as causes for the increase in cohabitation, the question still remains, why do cohabiting couples not marry? In the next section we will go on to examine how cohabiting partners themselves explain why they end up cohabiting, rather than getting married.

4 THE REASONS FOR COHABITATION

Our interviews and the BSA survey findings suggest that cohabitants are generally just as much committed to their partnerships, when we compare like with like, as married people. Some sort of dramatic spread in lack of commitment, therefore, cannot explain the increasing levels of cohabitation in Britain. Nor is ignorance of the law, in the form of widespread belief in the common law marriage myth, a satisfactory explanation for increasing cohabitation, as established earlier in the chapter. We are left, then, to consider alternative moralities and rationalities through which large numbers of people in Britain see cohabitation as an adequate way of conducting committed relationships with other adults, and of bringing up children.

We will approach this task through an analysis of the reasons given by cohabitants, in the interviews, to explain why they were cohabiting, rather than married. As we have seen, there are various types of cohabitation, and we will start with a tripartite classification, following the discussion in Prinz (1995), distinguishing between (1) cohabitation as a prelude to marriage, (2) cohabitation as a variety of marriage and (3) cohabitation as an alternative to marriage.

Cohabitation as a Prelude to Marriage

Cohabitation has often been viewed as a simple prelude to marriage: couples are simply trying out living together with marriage in mind. Successful unions are transformed into a legal and formal marriage; other partnerships just break up. While couples will have a commitment to one another, this is not the same as a long-term commitment. Consequent to this view, there would be little need, and little desire, for the extension of marriage-like legal rights to cohabitants.

It is indeed the case that it is now both statistically normal, and an expected norm, that couples will start living together through unmarried cohabitation. See chapter 2. We should be careful here to distinguish between the general, but vague, expectation that marriage might occur at some unspecified point in the future and a more conscious trial marriage. As chapter 2 also showed, most cohabitants in Britain see marriage as an ideal, sometimes a fairly abstract ideal, but also see living together unmarried as perfectly adequate for the everyday practicalities of partnering and parenting. This position is part of the experience of cohabitation as a variety of marriage. Rather, we are concerned for now with living together as preparation for marriage.

Many of our interviewees did indeed acknowledge this sort of cohabitation. Pamela, who married during the course of the research, put this most vividly:

> It's like going to buy a car, you don't go and buy a car without test driving it, would you, at the end of the day? That's the way I've felt. Live together, test each other out first, and you feel like you've done the hard work.

Gail, a nursery nurse with one daughter, expanded on what the trial consisted of:

> How can you know that you're going to like living with this person until you've lived with them. Everybody's got faults and they don't come out til you're living with them, so if you've gone out and got married and then gone to live with them it must be a big culture shock …

As chapter 2 shows, this view of the advantages of living together before marriage is widespread. But as chapter 2 also shows, this 'trial' period is often quite a long one. In the 2000 BSA survey, the mean duration of cohabitation was six and a half years, and only 20 per cent of current cohabitants had been living together for less than a year. In other words, most cohabitants live together much longer than any reasonable trial period. For partners would presumably have discovered most of each other's hidden faults after a year or so of 'test-driving'. For example Pamela and Gail, quoted above in expounding the benefits of cohabiting as trial marriage, had in fact both been cohabitants for eight years at the time of the interview. In such cases, cohabitation has progressed beyond a 'trial' to a committed long-term relationship. Formal marriage may remain an expectation, but is now just one part of the progression of the partnership, rather than a means of establishing and defining it.

Several of our interviewees described this evolutionary process as a relationship progressed from initial dating to committed, long-term co-residence. Marriage was more an incidental in this progress, rather than a defining marker. By the same token, it is important to remember that the reasons for entering a relationship are not necessarily the reasons why people stay in a relationship. In the terms of Table 4.1, initial contingent commitment can develop into mutual commitment. Judy, who had been cohabiting for 17 years and had two children, gave a striking retrospective account of the various stages through which her partnership had progressed. A first stage was 'drifting' into a more contingent partnership when a room became spare in a shared house:

what instigated the first move was the fact that I was sharing a house with somebody who decided to move in with her boyfriend and then got married and we decided to start renting together at that stage—that's it really, we've been together since.

At that stage she felt they were 'too young' to marry, but later she felt her mutual commitment with a partner did not need the formal stamp of marriage:

we've just never really felt the need to do that really; we've always been fairly committed to each other and just decide that, I can't even say that it was really a conscious decision ever, but just never ever got around to getting married really.

When children came, marriage was again discussed—mainly to please parents— although again not found necessary:

I do remember (parents) did ask me 'what if you decided to have children, what would you do then?' and I think we both said that we would think about marriage at that stage but when we did have children they were quite happy.

And now, 17 years later, her decision not to marry was seen as the right one:

from experience from friends who did live together and got married after being together for about 7–10 years, quite a few of my friends, they are divorced after marrying the person they lived with.

This evolution of cohabitation from trial marriage into a variety of marriage also fits in with the statistical evidence of union formation and dissolution. For if cohabitation was simply used as a preparation for marriage, then the number of marriages should increase, the divorce rate should decrease, and the cohabitating rate should remain roughly constant. None of these propositions is true. Both the behavioural and statistical evidence reviewed in this chapter show that 'trial' marriage often develops into a long-term variety of marriage.

Cohabitation as a Variety of Marriage

Most of our cohabiting interviewees saw themselves 'as good as married'. They may have begun to live together as a 'trial', or because of an unexpected pregnancy or housing problems, but that was some time ago and their relationship had now progressed to a long-term, committed partnership. Others became 'married' in this sense straight away. As Chris, who had been cohabiting for six years and had two daughters, explained:

We were just courting and decided we wanted to be more serious. Children were on the agenda straight away so we talked about it and decided to have the children straight away.

This was no principled alternative to marriage; rather cohabiting as if married was an alternative to remaining single. Angela, cohabiting for 13 years with one son, elaborated:

> We'd been together for about three years before we moved in together—I can't really remember how it came about but ... I wanted more commitment and he said right we'll live together.

Jane Lewis (2001) found much the same with her small sample of long-established partners with children. Most saw themselves as good as married, and could see little point in getting married now even if they did not reject marriage as an institution. Hence, as shown in the previous section, most interviewed cohabitants expressed and practiced levels of commitment in the same ways as demographically similar married couples (see Figure 4.1). Their union may not have been formalised by law, but for them that was a side-issue. Rather, their experience of cohabitation as a variety of marriage fitted in well with what we have called 'lived law' (see also chapter 3). Everyday social and institutional practice treats longer-term cohabitants, especially those with children, just like married couples. For some, this view was bolstered by belief in the existence of common law marriage. Diane, cohabiting for a year with two sons, one from a previous relationship, gives a good example:

> Being married is like living together, like boyfriend and girlfriend, it's just a ring on your finger. It's [cohabiting] just like being married really ... I feel as though I am, in a way, married because we ask each other if we can go out with friends or whatever—to me it is like I am married to him which I'm not. To me it's like being married without the ring and the certificate saying you are married—without the remembrance of a big party—I mean I can go and book a room and pretend I'm married and have a big party and say 'yes I'm married' but I'm not—it's just the same really. I don't feel like that at all, if we do ever split up it we'd sort things out, you see the child whenever, like you would if you were married, it's just to me as though I am married and I'm happy the way I am with him.

This is what we might call 'do-it-yourself' marriage. More grandly, to adapt from Bourdieu, this common type of cohabitation is a form of 'institutional bricolage' (Cleaver, 2002). People have taken existing institutional forms—in this case formal marriage and the lived law of 'living together as if married' (as the Inland Revenue puts it), combined them, and developed their own variety of marriage. They have responded to change by drawing on and adapting existing norms. This is partly to conserve cognitive and social energy—it is far harder to forge completely new institutions, as the pioneers of 1970s communes can testify. In so doing, people confer the new arrangements of 'common law marriage' with the legitimacy of tradition, and this therefore becomes part of 'the right way of doing things'. As we have seen, this do-it-yourself marriage does not exclude formal marriage at all and partners are not opposed to legal marriage. Indeed, why should they be when they perceive themselves to be as good as married? Rather, formal marriage is often seen more as an expectation, sometimes a rather vague and ideal expectation, for some future date.

In this case, if cohabiting partners were 'as good as married', then why bother with formal marriage at all, even as a vague expectation? There seem to be several linked reasons for this, which are all at bottom about public display, rather than private commitment. The first is to secure a name change, particularly if there are children, so that all members of the family share the same name. Many cohabitants see having a different surname from their partner and children as the greatest disadvantage of not marrying. In fact female name changing upon marriage is not a legal requirement, but rather a powerful tradition; nor is it illegal to take on your partner's name without marriage, or to choose a combined surname for children. This belief in the legal requirements for surname change appears as the converse to the common law marriage myth, therefore. The desire for a name change can also be linked to a feeling that this will complete the marriage-like partnership already bestowed through cohabitation. As Caroline, cohabiting for five years and with two sons, said:

> I think the only time I went through a phase [of wanting legal marriage] was the fact that they [children] are Williamsons—like they're part of him and I'm not, like I'm the odd one out. Like I wasn't complete, like there was something missing about me. Like we started this family yet I still wasn't 100% ... but I don't think like that now ...

For some respondents, especially those who did not believe in common law marriage, the ability to tidy up financial arrangements through legal marriage was also part of this desire to seal an already existing 'lived law' marriage. For example, Phillip, a 54 year-old plumber, had been cohabiting for two years. He was also a JP, which perhaps gave him more legal knowledge than most. Getting married the week after the interview, one reason was that:

> ... we felt that from that practical and legal point of view it's far easier to administer as a married couple. With buying and moving there are difficulties legally when you're not married in setting up things for your own children—there are difficulties like I'm living in her house at the moment and so we thought, apart from anything else that we wanted to get married, we also thought it would tidy up things and make it easier for us to do what we wanted for the future for our own children and grandchildren.

The major reason for wanting marriage, either as a vague expectation or as a practical plan, was for public performance and display. As most cohabitants saw themselves 'as good as married', there was no need for a cheap and easy register office marriage in order to mark their personal commitment. Rather, the respondents wanted a 'proper wedding' to show this publicly. Caroline explained:

> Probably somewhere in beautiful grounds, beautiful gardens, all outside, beautiful cars or horse drawn carriage—really spend a few grand on it and have a really fantastic day for him as well as for her. We could go to the Register Office up the road tomorrow if we wanted!

While Sophie, cohabiting for two and a half years with two children, wanted snow:

> It's supposed to be the best day of your life—you are the centre of atten- tion—you get what you want on your wedding day—I said to dad I wanted snow and he said 'You'll have snow if you want!'

As Chris noted, 'proper weddings' like this also mean substantial financial out- lay:

> We won't just opt for a cheap wedding … we'll wait until we can afford a proper wedding ... at the moment it's not the most important thing—the kids are the most important thing at the moment and we will get married when we can afford it. It's not that we don't want to get married, it's the financial side of it.

To see the wedding as public display is quite logical; after all it is a public occa- sion, as Mr Justice Lindsay reminded actress Catherine Zeta Jones in the High Court when in 2004 she sued for damages over unauthorised photographs of her wedding. There are, however, two crucial differences with earlier practice. One is the expense: display not only means marriage in public, but conspicuous con- sumption. Second, when partners often see themselves as already as good as married, marriage itself becomes reduced to the 'proper wedding'. This is remi- niscent of Tony Giddens' description of marriage as a 'shell institution' (Giddens, 1999) and of Ulrich Beck's notion of social institutions as 'zombie categories' which are 'dead and still alive' (Beck, 2002: 203). In this view the structural rea- sons which support a particular institution are fatally weakened, and enormous changes have taken place in what actually happens although the façade is seem- ingly unchanged. In this case marriage is no longer socially expected for partner- ship and childbearing, and relations within marriage are conducted in quite different ways from before, but the institution itself survives—emptied of its for- mer social content and now used for something quite different from before.

So if a 'proper wedding' is about display, what is this display about—what is being shown to friends and relatives? We might imagine that one motive is the desire to show personal commitment through public performance. In practice, this seems to be linked to a desire to show social success: marriage is no longer a rite of passage into adulthood as in the 1950s and 60s, but rather a rite of passage into the ranks of the socially successful. Personal commitment was part of this package. Many of our respondents were less circumspect and simply saw marriage as a means of showing off. Sharon, cohabiting for seven years with three children, had no thoughts of marriage and speculated:

> I suppose people try and outdo each other. I suppose it's keeping up with the Joneses'. If your friends get married and have a big white wedding then you probably want one bigger and better.

Philip, the JP shortly to be married, was more caustic:

> I feel that a young bride likes to have a big day to show off to her friends, her family and everybody else. 'Look, it's me, I'm getting married, we're going to spend £15,000–£20,000'—which is quite the norm now—Look at me, look at us.

Pamela, recently married herself but cohabiting for eight years with her husband to be before this, explained why showing off was so important, and why this meant expense:

> I think it's ever so important today because it's such a materialistic world. Everybody is trying to outdo everybody on everything. For example my wedding dress was £700 ... and I thought that was lot of money—a friend of mine who got married the other month, her dress was £2,500 and it was beautiful and everything but it's like everybody's trying to outdo everybody.

The wedding as public display, to be effective, costs a lot of money. This commodification of marriage as another consumer good, albeit one which is particularly useful in establishing social status, has certain economic consequences. Some people will not be able to afford the good and, for all, the good will be subject to opportunity costs. We found this to be a telling factor in the minds of many respondents (as did Eekelaar and Maclean, 2004). Sharon was therefore inclined to give formal marriage a miss:

> Expense is a major factor. It's not cheap to get married. We sat down and talked about it—it's not just Register Office or church, you've got to get clothes for the kids, clothes for us—it's a lot of money and what for—just for the certificate saying you're married—it's the same relationship if we were married, we've got children together, we've got bills together—if we had the sort of money to get married I'd rather take the children on holiday personally or he'd rather have a new car ...

Gail simply ranked marriage beneath other, more attractive, acquisitions:

> ... it's a case of we're looking now for a conservatory for the house and
> that's going to cost a lot more money. We want to start going on holidays and
> that's costing money, he says 'what would you rather have?'—a new car, we
> got a new car last year, it's 'what would you rather have, a new car or a wed-
> ding?' and now it's a conservatory.

Or as Tony, who was living in a flat with his partner of seven years, put it:

> you're looking at about £15,000 for a proper wedding and I'd rather spend
> that on a house.

For these cohabitants, who saw themselves as good as married, the legal side of
getting married formally—just like the legal side of not being married—remained
peripheral. The church or civil registration was just another part of the ritual on
which to hang the public display of a 'proper marriage'. They had no objections
to marriage, felt that the same norms were applicable to both cohabitation and
marriage, and even intended to formally marry eventually. Differences in commitment and behaviour in being a partner and parent between these couples and
demographically similar married couples are negligible. This sort of cohabitation
is a 'do-it-yourself' variety of marriage.

Cohabitation as an Alternative to Marriage

Cohabitation has sometimes been interpreted as an alternative to marriage. As
we have seen, for many of our interviewees this was not the case: living together unmarried was perceived rather as a long-term prelude to marriage or as a
variety of marriage. However, a significant minority of our first round respondents (16 out of 48) did see cohabitation as an alternative to marriage, in the
sense that they did not want to get married, even though they wanted to live with
and commit to a partner. There were two main reasons for using cohabitation as
an alternative to marriage. The first was a principled desire to escape patriarchy,
where marriage was seen as first and foremost a patriarchal institution; the second was disillusion with marriage as an effective institution. Not surprisingly,
these reasons can overlap.

   Naomi, who had never married but had been cohabiting for 15 years and had
two children, gave a clear articulation of the escaping patriarchy view:

> I also didn't want to for political reasons because I thought it was really good
> that we didn't have to anymore because of the symbolism of a woman being
> a man's property. A married woman had no rights in her own property at all,
> she lost all her rights when she got married and I totally disagree with that—
> it's a very good reflection of my independence and being with one another
> that we don't have to get married. Personally I would see it as a great defeat
> if I got married.

For others, being married in the past had encouraged this 'political' view of marriage; their experiences had shown them that marriage was a form of male control. Natalie, now cohabiting for three years with two children from her previous marriage, listed how this proceeded:

> He tried to control me all the time. When I first started work he didn't want me to have a job or want me to learn to drive and things like that. I needed to, I needed to go to work and I needed to learn to drive because of the children and school and things like that and shopping.

While Natasha, cohabiting for 12 years with three daughters, saw marriage negatively in terms of ownership:

> Living together you get on better. You really do—with marriage you own each other—with that bit of paper you are tied no matter what but living together it's easier—you are easier with each other and you haven't got that piece of paper hovering over your head all the time—you haven't got that ball and chain on your finger. He doesn't say to me you've got my ring on your finger I own you, you're mine, there's none of that.

Not surprisingly, perhaps, these views were apparently more common in the small sample of separated cohabitants interviewed by Charlie Lewis and colleagues (2002), as compared to our wider-ranging sample. In this case, two-thirds of the sample described marriage in negative terms, focusing on an antipathy to control by church and state and institutionalised sexism. For them, as with our respondents in this group, cohabitation offered the better way to commit to a partner— and to end a relationship—in an egalitarian way free of externally imposed rules.

Other cohabitants in our sample had not drawn wider conclusions about marriage as an inegalitarian institution, but were disillusioned with marriage—it was a failing or dangerous institution. There was a strong possibility of breakdown and the costs of this were high. Paula, cohabiting for three years with one son, was nine years old when her parents divorced. Her grandparents had broken up before she was born and her aunt and uncle were divorced too. She does not altogether rule out marriage, but:

> It just makes you a bit more aware—even though you meet somebody at say, 16 and you live together, have your children, it doesn't always work that you live happily ever after ...

As Kate, cohabiting for three years with one daughter, pointed out, a failed marriage would be both unpleasant and costly: 'you'd have to go through a horrible divorce and that again can cost money', while Amanda, who had experienced a painful divorce but had now been cohabiting for seven years, with two daughters, focused on the emotional costs:

> then when it starts getting nasty you have to give them an issue to be nasty
> back, you know and, like adultery, blah, blah, blah, and it's like, you've got
> an open wound and when you're having to put it down on paper and then
> having to get the letters and that, it's like you're ripping it all open again. You
> never seem to get over it.

It is these likely costs of a quite possible breakdown that may help to explain why
a high proportion of cohabitants—up to a third according to John Haskey
(2001)—are either divorced, or separated from spouses. Finally, we saw in the
last section that marriage, in the form of a 'proper wedding', is used as a type of
social status display. But this display can easily be double-edged, as breakdown
will also be on display. Duncan was particularly concerned about this:

> it's the public thing so if it goes wrong there's a lot of public statements as
> well, sort of public failure if the marriage goes wrong which might be a
> background thing which is affecting the way I'm thinking.

Respondents in this group saw marriage in negative terms, and cohabitated as an
alternative to it. These respondents were also among the more 'liberal' in their
evaluation of cohabitation. For example, none of these interviewees thought that
married couples make better parents than unmarried couples. This group probably includes more divorced and separated people, who have negative personal
experience of marriage, as well as those who take a more principled and political
stand against marriage as an institution. In this aversion to marriage they differ
from the other two types of cohabitants, those using cohabitation as 'trial marriage' and those who see living together as a variety of marriage. It is the two latter groups, however, who will make up the majority of cohabitants.

5 CONCLUSION: VIRTUAL AND REAL FAMILIES IN POLICY-MAKING

Cohabitants seem to show just as much commitment to their partnerships, when
we compare like with like, as married people. Some cohabitants are less committed than others, but the same goes for married people. Some sort of dramatic
spread in lack of commitment, therefore, cannot explain the increasing levels of
cohabitation in Britain. Nor is ignorance of the law, in the form of widespread
belief in the common law marriage myth, a satisfactory explanation for increasing cohabitation.

Rather, we find that large numbers of people in Britain perceive and experience
cohabitation as a type of marriage. First, the majority now experience cohabitation as a prelude to marriage. However, 'marriage' in this case does not necessarily mean formal, legally registered marriage, for increasingly longer-term

cohabitation is seen as a variety of marriage—such cohabitants are 'as good as married'. Even many of the minority who are opposed to marriage, either for reasons of principle or because of practical disillusionment, are in effect practising a variety of a marriage. Cohabitation is experienced as an adequate way of conducting committed relationships with other adults, and of bringing up children. Cohabitants are not acting irrationally, therefore, although many are left in a less secure legal position than married spouses. Nor should we forget the rapid changes occurring in formal marriage itself, where re-evaluation of the partnership is increasingly taken for granted and, consequently, where divorce has become a functional necessity, almost a part of the life course. It is perhaps more accurate to say that marriage is a variety of cohabitation. Both cohabitants and married spouses are attempting to work out how to combine personal freedom with commitment to others. In this way it is quite wrong to see the statistical decrease in marriage, and the rise in unmarried cohabitation, as leading to or reflecting the 'breakdown of the family'.

Cohabitation and marriage are not diametrically opposed, therefore, nor (as shown also in chapter 2) do cohabitants and married spouses belong to different tribes. In fact, this research, like other studies (for example J Lewis, 2001; Eekelaar and Maclean, 2004) shows that demographically similar cohabitants and married spouses are often indistinguishable. As Kathleen Kiernan and Valerie Estaugh pointed out as long ago as 1993, there are more differences between different types of marriage, and between different types of cohabitation, than between them. Unfortunately, much legal and policy discourse has not gone inside the black boxes; in focusing on outward distinctions in the legal form of families—on cohabitation versus marriage—this debate has neglected the social content—what families actually do. The similarities between cohabitation and marriage have thereby been missed. In this way policy has instead become fixated on attributing family dysfunctionality by form, where cohabitation is seen as the inferior partnership form. It is as if policy has addressed what John Gillis (1985) has called 'virtual families', the ideal, fairy-tale families portrayed in Christmas cards and wedding magazines—and indeed in the 'proper wedding' so desired by many of our interviewees—rather than the real families of everyday life. As one of our interviewees, Bethan, put it:

> In the nice fairytale world it would be nice to meet somebody and fall in love and live happily ever after but life doesn't happen like that. I wish it did.

This is perhaps the true 'marriage myth', a romanticised and increasingly commercialised version of romantic love (Evans, 2003). Rather, policy should focus on how partners can best exercise their care and commitment towards each other and their children. In this respect cohabitation and marriage are little different. The next chapter turns to an evaluation of what legal reforms might address the world of these real families.

5

Changing Law: Social Attitudes to Cohabitation Law, Law Reform and the Legal Response

1 INTRODUCTION

Chapter 4 has identified the divergence between 'virtual' families and 'real' families. Virtual families are an idealised notion attractive to policy makers (among others) which pictures a happy and committed marriage for life, while for 'real' families—married or unmarried—commitment and happiness is spread along a spectrum and variously shaped by the real life context in which they are lived. From the law-maker's point of view, diverse and changing real families are of course much more difficult to legislate for and easier to ignore where possible. Such ambivalence to changing social reality has led the law to develop unevenly in its attempts to grapple with social change in the family sphere. This is particularly the case where the legal position of cohabitants is concerned. As we have seen in chapter 1, in some areas of law cohabitants are equated with the married, in others they are regulated as a family inferior to their married counterparts, and in yet other contexts they are treated as strangers.

The focus of this chapter will be a consideration of the tension between prevailing social attitudes and cohabitation and marriage law. This is exacerbated by rapidly changing social norms (see chapter 2) and the ambivalent response of legal policy makers in England and Wales to the unmarried cohabiting family. For the social phenomenon of family structuring away from marriage—or *démariage* (Théry, 1994)—challenges the legitimacy of marriage-centred family law regulation which still, at the turn of the century, prevails in Britain. In particular, the significance of the divergence between social and legal norms will be examined, leaving an assessment of the options for legal reform to the next chapter.

2 THE PROBLEMATIC EFFECTS OF THE CURRENT LAW

As we have seen from the discussion on the pervasive nature of the common law marriage myth in chapter 3, the different legal treatment of heterosexual cohabitants as compared with married couples set out in chapter 1 is not understood by the majority of people in Britain. This leaves many couples to arrange their legal affairs on a false premise. Many assume, quite wrongly, that the family law protection and rights afforded to married couples on divorce or death or in respect of their children apply equally to cohabiting couples and that no independent action on their part is called for. Our interviews with cohabitants and former cohabitants alike confirmed that formal legal advice was rarely sought and was thought of as something to be obtained only when things went wrong, at which point, in fact, it will usually be too late to achieve a marriage-like settlement. Sharon, 34, cohabiting for eight years and with two children, indicated the general reluctance to approach solicitors when asked if she had ever taken advice about her position as a cohabitant:

> No. If we ever did split up then I suppose I would have to get legal advice but I would just want to walk away ...

Kevin, a 45 year old engineer and previously married, had been cohabiting for 5 years and had one young child of the relationship. In response to the same question, he also stressed that this is not something to be done when the relationship is going well:

> No—I would imagine the situation arises only when a couple who are cohabiting are not on the best terms—I suppose that's when people start thinking about what their rights are—what's mine, what's theirs, how would I stand if it went to Court ...

The certainty of the majority of cohabitants that the law recognises them as married was captured in many of our interviews, and revealed a surprising depth of conviction that this is how the law treated them. Angela, a 37 year old Birmingham store manager, who had cohabited for some 13 years, typified the response of this group. When asked if cohabiting and married couples had the same legal rights, she confirmed,

> Oh yes definitely, the same yes. ... Oh yes, you've got the same legal rights.

More worryingly still, even where the legal position is appreciated, few cohabitants who do not believe in the existence of common law marriage take the legal steps required to redress the position of disadvantage, for example by making a will or a parental responsibility agreement. As noted in chapter 4, only 15 per cent of those who rightly did not believe their partner had automatic inheritance rights (as opposed to nine percent who did) had made or changed a will as a result of cohabiting. Similarly, more correct legal knowledge did not at all affect the already low probability of couples entering into a parental responsibility agreement (five per cent) or making a legal declaration about shares in a family home not purchased jointly (nine per cent). Thus a policy of better informing people of their rights would not necessarily ensure that appropriate advice and action was taken.

Our follow-up interviews did reveal, however, that there may often be good intentions to undertake the legal steps necessary to gain outcomes and protection similar to those automatically given to married couples. Reasons given in our interviews for not taking these steps were various. They included the cost of legal advice, the complexity or multiplicity of the arrangements which need to be made, general inertia or a perceived lack of urgency about the need to put arrangements in place. Thus Lynda, from whom we heard in chapter 4, who had cohabited for over eight years, had two children with her partner but was still married to someone else, knew a will should be made and that she needed legal advice. Yet the high cost of legal services meant she had delayed taking appropriate action and was trying to do her own legal research to minimise the legal costs. Naomi, who had been cohabiting with her partner, the father of her two children, for some 15 years in a property of which she was the sole owner was also aware of the need to make a will. Yet in the busy schedule of their daily lives within a secure and marriage-like relationship, she had taken no action to ensure that her partner could remain with their children unchallenged in the family home, should she die. As she explains,

> No. We haven't done any sort of planning like that in the relationship. It's been very much day to day. That's why I still haven't written a Will.

Were they married and she had died leaving no will, her estate would have passed automatically to her partner who would have had automatic parental responsibility for their children and been exempt from paying inheritance tax. As things stand, if Naomi were to die the home would pass on intestacy to be held on trust for the two children, subject to any claim her partner may have had under a constructive trust in property law or as a cohabitant under the Inheritance (Provision for Family and Dependants) Act 1975 for limited financial provision. Given the value of the home, Naomi's children and partner would probably—unlike a married spouse—have to pay inheritance tax on any property they receive on her death, which would significantly reduce the value of their inheritance and may mean they had to sell the home to pay the tax.

Similarly, Paul, who has two children by a previous relationship, is not overly concerned about not having made a will despite the potential for conflict between his partner and his children were he to die. The family home where he lives with his partner and their child was bought in his sole name. If he dies without having made a will, his estate will be divided equally between his three children. His partner and youngest child would have no automatic right to stay in their home. This result could only be achieved if she were to make a claim under the Inheritance (Provision for Family and Dependants) Act 1975 for her financial provision which would be limited to her maintenance but which would naturally reduce the share of the estate, which would otherwise go to the children. This would clearly be a very difficult position in which to leave his partner. Yet Paul's optimism prevented him from confronting this situation and enabled him to put matters off, claiming

> ... I don't plan on going anywhere anyway yet!

Thus currently, the law leaves cohabitants (for whom there will usually be no retrospective route back to agree arrangements) in a legal quagmire of child law, property law and/or succession law when their relationship ends. This compares badly with the position of the married for whom the law provides relatively straightforward rights and remedies based on cohesive family law principles. The majority of cohabitants are unaware of their legal vulnerability and among those that are aware, few are spurred into putting legal arrangements in place. Whilst the law assumes that people will undertake 'private ordering' (Mnookin, 1979) to plug the gaps left by the different treatment of married and cohabiting families, this does not seem to be happening on any scale. This may of course be because cohabitants do not wish to take such action, as they do not want to put themselves as nearly as possible in the same position as married couples, and undoubtedly some cohabitants will take this view. However, as the quote above suggests, this does not seem to be the intention of the majority of 'legally aware' but inactive cohabitants, still less of the majority who believed in the legal existence of common law marriage. As chapter 4 showed, cohabitants are likely to be just as committed to one another and their partnership and children as demographically similar married spouses. How, then, do people think the law should treat cohabiting families?

3 ATTITUDES TO COHABITATION AND MARRIAGE LAW

The BSA survey found a pervasive belief in the legal existence of common law marriage and exposed the confusion surrounding how this operates. As discussed in chapter 3, people partly believed in the existence of common law marriage because it fitted in with what they thought was logical and morally sensible from the point of view of family responsibilities. This was why they were much more likely to believe in the legal power and efficacy of common law marriage where children and parents were concerned, as opposed to property issues. In like manner, the BSA survey found clear support, amongst both cohabitants and the wider population, for reform of the law to assimilate the rights of married and unmarried couples when respondents were asked what they thought the legal situation ought to be.

In putting forward scenarios where the law treated married and unmarried couples differently, we found that key aspects of the current law were considered unjust. All survey respondents were asked about three issues where the law discriminates against cohabitants. Firstly, they were asked to consider the issue of maintenance on relationship breakdown in the following scenario:

> I'd now like you to imagine an unmarried couple with no children who have
> been living together for ten years. Say their relationship ends. Do you think
> the woman should or should not have the same rights as a married woman to
> claim financial support from the man, or should she have fewer rights?

A clear majority of this representative sample, 61 per cent, thought she should have the same rights, although over a third (37 per cent) thought she should not, with only two per cent being unsure (see Q1 in the bar-chart of Figure 5.1 below). Among cohabitants, however, the number in favour of her having the right to financial support rose to 70 per cent. Thus a clear majority felt marriage-like treatment to be appropriate in this context.

In our follow-up interviews, seven of the 17 current cohabitants were clearly in favour of the extension of maintenance rights to cohabitants. These interviews allow us to explore why cohabitants thought this way about the law. Thus Kate had been living with her partner for three years at the time of the interview and thought that the right to claim financial support post-separation should be equally available to female cohabitants because they had done the same job as a married woman:

> ... because she's played the same role hasn't she as if she was married?
> She's done everything the same as she would do if they were married so
> therefore she's put the same into it.

Colin said that he would fight his partner if she did claim anything but nonetheless saw a similar social logic after twelve months of cohabitation,

> Yeah, it should be the same. ...Yeah ... I'd still fight against it, like.

Others were less sure about the appropriateness of maintenance in both the married and the unmarried contexts, particularly where there were no children of the relationship or where the relationship was short term. Emily didn't think maintenance should follow relationship breakdown at all, stating:

> I didn't realise that if you were married and had children and got divorced, I didn't realise you could get financial support.

Caroline, reflecting the view of several respondents, is adamant that in contrast to those who have children, a cohabitant without children should not receive maintenance:

> If they've got no children, then no. She's big enough and ugly enough to look after herself if she hasn't got any children. Fair enough if she's dedicated her life, given her life up so to speak, to be with him and have kids and he's just decided to part then she's going to need a certain amount of help because she's been used to a certain way of living but if they've got no kids then definitely not, she can look after herself, she can start again ...

Amanda was unconvinced about the need for maintenance generally, but acknowledged that the length of the relationship, the age of the parties and the way in which it broke down might combine to make some sort of compensation appropriate:

> Say she was 50 and say she'd give it 30 years ... and he'd decided to get a younger model then perhaps he should give her some financial pay-off.

From these responses we can see that the theme of social logic exposed in chapter 3, in relation to beliefs about common law marriage, is continued. Respondents tended to see that the law should treat maintenance issues in line with what they thought morally right in the family context. In this case, maintenance should be more assured if there were children involved and/or if the partnership was long-standing. This implies that it is the functional similarity of married and cohabiting families, rather than their formal difference, that is the basis upon which it was felt the law should operate.

Opinions about the division of assets on death were almost uniform in favour of marriage-like rights. Our second scenario put to respondents in the BSA survey asked whether people thought the same cohabitant of ten years should or should not be able to remain in the family home after the death of her partner. Here overall 93 per cent thought she should, six per cent thought she should not and one per cent were unsure (see Q2 in the bar-chart of Figure 5.1 below). Again, among cohabitants those in favour of marriage-like treatment rose, this time to 97 per cent. Our cohabiting interviewees were also more uniformly in favour of a right to succeed to the family home. Amanda felt here that the surviving partner should be able to have the home:

> Yes, ... because he's died. ... They'd built that house together, hadn't they?
> I mean, if ... he or she had walked out it's a different scenario but if some-
> one dies, then it should be whoever's the living one takes it on.

Emily was also in favour of the women partner in this scenario being able to stay
in the home (if they had been living together for five to six years), despite being
adamant that the woman in scenario 1 should not be able to claim maintenance.

> I'd say yes to that but then that goes completely against what I've just said
> but it's different—you haven't just upped and walked away.

A clear consensus exists in favour of the law facilitating the automatic succession
of a cohabitant to the family home vested in the sole name of their deceased partner where no will has been made. Here again, we find that respondents imply a
social logic which depends upon ideas of fairness to individuals while sustaining
families.

Finally, we asked respondents to consider the position of the cohabiting father
in the following scenario:

> Now imagine an unmarried couple who have been living together for ten
> years. They have a child who needs medical treatment. Do you think the
> father should or should not have the same rights as a married man to make
> decisions about his child's medical treatment as he would if he was married
> to the child's mother?

A resounding 97 per cent thought he should (rising to 99 per cent among cohabitants), two per cent thought he should not, and one per cent were unsure (see Q3
in Figure 5.1 below). In fact, since we carried out this research, the law has been
amended to give parental responsibility to all unmarried fathers, whether cohabiting or not, who jointly register the birth of their child with the mother.
However, this is not retrospective and applies only to children born on or after 1
December 2003 (s111 Adoption and Children Act 2002, amending s4 Children
Act 1989). It therefore still leaves unmarried fathers of older children and any
father who does not jointly register the birth without any automatic formal legal
status in respect of his child, regardless of the extent of their role in the child's
upbringing.

We did not find any systematic social differences in attitudes to law reform, as
indicated by the responses to these scenario questions. There were no significant
differences in the responses of men and women, by people of different ages, or
by those in different occupational or class groups, as revealed by the BSA survey.
Nor was ethnic origin a factor in shaping people's ideas about the law or how it
should be reformed, as shown by the follow-up interviews. The attitudes
expressed by the African-Caribbean sample towards law reform were almost

FIGURE 5.1 *Should Cohabitants have the Same Rights as Married Couples?*

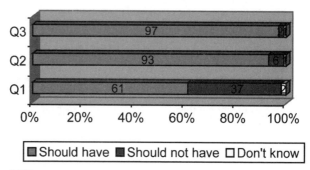

Source: BSA Survey, 2000.

identical to respondents in the BSA survey (as in fact with all other issues). More surprisingly, the Asian respondents also favoured the assimilation of unmarried and married couples' legal rights, even though the majority of them would not countenance cohabiting outside marriage themselves. This is perhaps reflective of a sort of 'cultural bilingualism'. Jamal for example was emphatic:

> Why? ... I mean, why should a married couple have more rights than an unmarried couple, right? There is no difference... because they're married, it doesn't mean they can have more rights than a non-married couple.

Khulsoom also perceived anything other than equal treatment as unjust:

> [Otherwise] it's just not fair. It's not fair to the unmarried people.

However, the extension of automatic marriage-like rights, although popular, were not necessarily seen as the only or best option. Some of those interviewed demonstrated an awareness of the need for flexibility in order to accommodate the variety of family structures in Britain, as Caroline suggested when she said that,

> There's different things about different people though—what situation is good for one couple might not be for another couple.

It would be important in considering the options for law reform to take this need for flexibility into account.

Overall, therefore, we have found that the population at large and the cohabiting population in particular favour the extension of marriage-based rights to cohabitants in the contexts suggested in the scenarios. Some have suggested that to impose marriage-like law on cohabitants would be an oppressive rather than a liberating act by law-makers (Deech, 1980; Freeman, 1984, cf Bailey-Harris, 1996). We found that this was not seen to be the case for the large majority. Our study also exposes a general belief in the need for law reform in this area to give cohabitants marriage-like legal rights, although as discussed in the next chapter we found varying opinions as to when such legal rights should begin.

4 THE FUNCTIONAL CONVERGENCE OF MARRIAGE AND COHABITATION—SHOULD WE REGULATE FAMILY FUNCTION OR FAMILY FORM?

Family law has traditionally been regulated according to a family's status or form, reinforcing the moral superiority and desirability of marriage by according it legal privilege. Conversely, unmarried families were largely ignored until the 1970s, when we saw the beginning of a more neutral approach to family regulation (Glendon, 1980). Before this unmarried mothers and their children were deliberately and uniformly stigmatised by the humiliating procedures through which child maintenance was obtained (as with the Affiliation Act 1957 (repealed by the Family Law Act 1987) under which the unmarried mother's uncorroborated evidence of paternity was inadmissible). The public attitudes which now prevail towards law reform, as revealed in the last section, shows how this view of unmarried cohabitation no longer receives public backing.

In the past it could be argued that the traditional approach of the law in discounting, ignoring and undermining unmarried cohabitation had accorded with prevailing attitudes at that time, backed up as they were by a strong social and religious ethos favouring marriage. Marriage was the only normatively acceptable way through which to partner and parent, at least since the rise of Victorian values in the mid nineteenth century (although as we have seen in chapter 4 many people continued to live outside these norms). However, as the last section and chapters 2 and 4 have shown, this is no longer the case. Socially, unmarried cohabitation is widely practised and accepted within British society as a partnering and parenting structure; certainly cohabitants are no longer stigmatised. The number of couples electing to cohabit is rising fast, as is the average duration of cohabitation relationships. Indeed, cohabitation as trial marriage is seen as a positive, even necessary, thing to do and there is little social pressure to acquire married status even for the purpose of childbearing. Trial marriage often continues to become a variety of marriage, as most longer-term cohabitants see themselves as good as married and just as committed to their partners and their families as married spouses. Nor are married parents generally considered to make better parents than unmarried parents. While marriage is still highly valued as an ideal, and many cohabitants expect to marry at some time, the decision to marry or cohabit has become more of a personal choice in which the legal significance of the couple's actions does not figure highly, if at all. Indeed for many, marriage has become equated with an expensive 'proper wedding' used to display social standing and status, rather than a passport to adulthood or respectability. For most cohabitants see themselves as good as married in terms of personal commitment and public acceptability. Whether to marry or cohabit has become a personal decision made in the context of a couple's own lives.

This switch in the decision whether to marry or not to being a personal lifestyle choice, rather than externally imposed duty, is in part explained by the fact that marriage itself has changed. First of all, marriage has become 'companionate': ideally a partnership of emotional equals, in which each partner is expected to support and help the other achieve personal fulfilment (Beck-Gernsheim, 2002). These conditions are harder to achieve, which makes marriage more likely to break down. In any case, part of the new 'marriage contract' is that it endures only as long as both partners wish it to continue; it is ended easily and without stigma by divorce, at which point there is a non-fault-based redistribution of family assets backed up by a system of welfare benefits. As we saw in chapter 4, given the social changes to marriage as an institution, easy divorce is now a functional necessity without which it could barely continue. Marriage is therefore no longer the life-long patriarchal institution from which there was little or no chance of escape for either spouse and especially the financially dependent wife. In effect we are witnessing a 'functional convergence' of married and unmarried cohabitation. Unmarried cohabitation has taken on many of the functions of marriage, displacing shotgun weddings and formal engagements as well as providing companionship, emotional support, sexual intimacy, financial interdependence and a site for homemaking and parenting. At the same time marriage has in many ways become more like cohabitation: it is increasingly a negotiated partnership, not necessarily involving financial dependency, which may be terminated almost at will. These social changes have been accompanied by legal changes, for example to divorce law. In these ways the distinctiveness of the married state, and of marriage as an institution, have become far less obvious and important. But there is still a massive legal contradiction in this whole gamut of social change—it is marriage alone which offers consistent legal privilege.

The first question for legal policy makers must therefore be why we regulate marriage in this way at all. Is it because of its *form*—a state-endorsed contractual arrangement embodying a public commitment which is potentially life-long and which accordingly justifies compensation on early termination by divorce or death? As we have seen, this is hardly a picture of real marriage, but policy makers may argue that this is nevertheless a social ideal which deserves legal canonisation. Or is it because of the *function and effects of marriage*, namely that it is a joint enterprise of sexual intimacy, companionship, emotional and financial support, homemaking, childbearing and child rearing, which is essential to society as a whole but which distorts the bargaining power, needs and resources of the individual parties who therefore should be legally protected? In the past, or at least after the mid nineteenth century when marriage became a social norm for all from which it was difficult to deviate, form and function roughly coincided.

Consequently, these questions were far less pressing. Family law thereby developed to protect a partner prejudiced by the functions and effects of family life on divorce or death of the other partner (typically the woman)—but uniquely within the legal form of marriage. Until recently, there was no need to identify which aspects of marriage provided the rationale for such protection and privilege. However, given that the functions and effects of marriage are now also sited within unmarried cohabitation relationships (and vice-versa), another question becomes acute for policy makers. Can we continue to justify confining this protective legal privileging to marriage alone?

5 THE LEGAL RESPONSE TO SOCIAL NORMS

A key aspect of what may be termed the 'function versus form' debate within family law must be the interaction between social and legal norms. In particular, should or can the imposition of legal norms be used effectively to change social norms and thus social behaviour in this context? Or are the new social norms so powerful that the only realistic legal response is to regulate families according to their function and effects? Certainly the social and religious norms which made marriage for life a prerequisite to a family's social acceptance have largely disappeared. In their place is a new flexibility and tolerance concerning family structure within which any legal distinctions between the married and unmarried cohabiting states are often blurred or deemed irrelevant to people's lives (see chapter 4). The social function and effects of partnering and parenting within either family are similar. Ironically, aside from the public statement of commitment made at a wedding—which as we saw in chapter 4 is often more a matter of performance than principle—it is now only the legal distinctions between married and unmarried cohabitation that set these two family forms apart. Unfortunately, as we saw in chapter 3, relatively few people in general (38 per cent in the 2000 BSA survey) and even fewer cohabitants (35 per cent) or parents (36 per cent) are aware of these all-important legal distinctions. And even where people were aware of the different legal implications, for the vast majority the legal advantages of marriage did not provide any 'good' reason to marry, as we saw in chapter 4. In most cases people's alternative rationalities about partnering and parenting mean that legal considerations do not feature strongly in the decision to marry or cohabit outside marriage.

However, despite this, policy makers and consequently the legislature remain confused as to how best to respond to the social acceptance and increasing practice of cohabitation. On one level, it is acknowledged that 'families do not want to be lectured about their behaviour or what kind of relationship they are in' (Home Office, 1998: para 4.2). And in some situations the law, as demonstrated in chapter 1, has been amended in a piecemeal fashion to treat cohabitants in a similar if not equal way to their married counterparts. This amounts to some acknowledgement of the need for a functional approach to legal reform. Yet on another level, it has been made clear that marriage is still the preferred family structure, at least where children are involved. Marriage is officially presented as the best means of ensuring family stability (see chapter 4 for the statistical and social weakness of this argument). Viewed from this angle, marriage is something that needs to be preserved and promoted, as stated in the Labour Government's 1998 blueprint for family policy, *Supporting Families*:

> [M]arriage does provide a strong foundation for stability for the care of children. It also sets out rights and responsibilities for all concerned. It remains the choice of the majority of people in Britain. For all these reasons, it makes sense for the Government to do what it can to strengthen marriage. (Home Office, 1998: para 4.8)

On the other hand cohabitation was not considered in any detail in this policy document. The only possible solution left to the complex legal position of cohabitants (other than the implicit advice that they should marry) is one of private ordering rather than state intervention (Barlow and Duncan, 2000). The paper's only direct suggestion was that 'it might therefore be worthwhile' to produce a guide for cohabitants setting out their legal rights in relation to income, property, tax, welfare benefits, and responsibility towards their children, to be made available in Citizens Advice Bureaux and libraries (para 4.15). This is echoed in the current campaign by the Department for Constitutional Affairs, following publication of the results from the BSA 2000 survey, to inform cohabitants of their lack of legal rights. These measures will do nothing at all to address the complexity and inadequacies of the law relating to cohabitation.

There has been little apparent development since 1998 in government thinking on different-sex cohabitants. This is in some contrast to the Labour Government's commitment to the ending of discrimination against same-sex couples who are unable to marry, by permitting them to enter into marriage-like registered civil partnerships (DTI Women and Equality Unit, 2003a; Queen's Speech, 2003; Civil Partnerships Act 2004). In this instance government policy seems to follow a 'functional' approach to family regulation. Same-sex couples perform similar roles to married couples, and so need similar legal rights. In contrast, legal discrimination against heterosexual cohabitants (and indeed unregistered same-sex cohabitants) is to continue, with only a need to provide them with better information about legal disadvantage being acknowledged (DTI Women and Equality Unit, 2003b: paras 3.5–3.6). Yet even this small concession to the pervasiveness of cohabitation does not address the general reluctance, and the practical barriers, cohabitants experience in obtaining and acting on legal advice even when they are aware of their inferior legal position. Here the Government appears to be further endorsing the form approach to family regulation—roles and functions are ignored, it is the ideal of marriage which is to be promoted.

Given the inconsistency and complexity in the legal regulation of cohabitants described in chapter 1, the wide social acceptance of cohabitation as shown in chapter 2, and the moral logic which people ascribe to family law as shown in chapters 4 and 5, it is much easier for people to believe that the law has by now taken on board the well-established practice of cohabitation as a family structure, than it is to believe the convoluted, and apparently illogical, legal truth. As Eekelaar has observed, paralleling our own discussion of cohabitation as 'lived law' in chapter 3:

> [I]n practice social rules may be as significant as legal rules. They may provide equal, or even more compelling, motives for action. ... For the purpose of living his or her life, the citizen may not care to spend too much time distinguishing between 'social' and 'legal' norms. The vagueness and indeterminancy of many social norms does not lessen their impact. Indeed, it may make their recognition and analysis even more urgent. (Eekelaar, 2000: 16)

If, as we saw in chapter 4, the majority of longer-term cohabitants, especially those with children, see themselves as good as married, and this is largely socially accepted in both institutional and social life, then how can policy makers use the law to enforce a form based view of marriage versus cohabitation? We suspect that to change social norms on this scale would take far more than a public information campaign; indeed if there was any chance of such legal intervention being effective at all it would become oppressive (much like the legal ban on divorce in Ireland up to 1995). This does not seem to be a likely or sensible road to take.

6 THE LEGAL ASSIMILATION OF COHABITATION, OR THE RENORMALISATION OF MARRIAGE?

As we have seen in chapter 1, during the 1970s and 1980s a process of legal assimilation of the rights and remedies of married and cohabiting couples took place. However, this process has to some extent been reversed with greater legal distinctions being made between cohabitation and marriage, for example, the remedies available in respect of domestic violence and occupation of the family home in Part IV Family Law Act 1996. For the New Labour government, marriage also remains the ideal family form and the 'renormalisation' of marriage, and the promotion of marriage, remains part of their family policy rhetoric. But as we have seen, a big question mark hangs over whether marriage can be successfully promoted through legal and policy initiatives when social norms no longer see marriage as an imperative or even desirable. Would the reassertion of pro-marriage legal norms alongside a high profile public information campaign, in the face of the decline of religious adherence and changed social norms about acceptable family structures, have the power to re-establish marriage as a social requisite? Would fear of legal vulnerability send people to the altar or alternatively to legal advisors? And would it make any difference if it did? Because of course if you haven't got a committed relationship to begin with, or even if you have, the vicar and a party aren't going to make much difference. Certainly the government is going part of the way along this course of action. A high profile publicity campaign to be conducted by the Advice Services Alliance under the guidance of the Department for Constitutional Affairs was launched on 15 July 2004 with the aim of raising awareness of the legal disadvantages of cohabitation as compared with marriage.

This marriage-promotion approach is built on the assumption that if law continues to privilege marriage and denies equivalent family law rights and protection to unmarried cohabitants, then people—if they are made aware of the position—will act 'rationally' and will respond by marrying in greater numbers. This will in turn, it is assumed, restore marriage as the social norm and create more stable families, thereby benefiting British society as a whole. As we saw in chapter 4, both of these assumptions rest on dubious grounds. First, people do not normally act in this legally rational way; although 'law is a purposive activity and policy makers expect results' (Maclean and Eekelaar, 1997: 7), legal considerations appear quite peripheral in most cases in the decision to marry or cohabit. Second, if we compare like with like, married couples are not notably more stable than cohabiting families. Certainly it is not the marriage certificate which creates stability, but the partnership itself. In addition, promoting marriage in effect means denigrating other family forms. Nor are cohabitants some discrete 'underclass' (Murray, 1994; Morgan, 1999), or a set of bohemian intellectuals, who can be either stigmatised or safely ignored by policy and law-makers. They are now, as chapters 2 and 4 show, a widespread, increasing and accepted part of the social fabric of British and indeed European society. Over the course of a lifetime, people are now likely to experience a variety of family forms suiting their particular situation at any given time. In many ways, therefore, any attempt to renormalise marriage by using family law to continue to regulate families according to form is a high risk strategy. It may very well fail, and if not it may turn out to be oppressive. What risks are involved in an alternative approach?

Another reaction would be for the law to regulate all families on a functional basis—that is according to what a family does rather than the legal form or status it takes.[1] Such a functional approach, implemented successfully in among other countries Australia and Canada, would consistently extend to all cohabiting families the provisions which currently apply to similarly constituted married families. In particular, this would arise where the relationship ends and would extend

---

[1] This dichotomy was nicely encapsulated by Ward LJ who, in attempting to distil what defines a family, concluded that for Rent Act tenancy succession purposes at least, 'The question is more what a family does than what a family is.' (See the dissenting judgment of Ward LJ in the Court of Appeal decision in *Fitzpatrick v Sterling Housing Association* [1997] 4 All ER 991.)

to cohabitants with or without children the existing discretionary redistribution of the married family's assets on divorce (or death of a married partner) in accordance with family law criteria. These take into account the length of the relationship, the needs of the parties, their resources and both financial and non-financial contributions to the welfare of the family (see s25 Matrimonial Causes Act 1973 and s3(2) Inheritance (Provision for Family and Dependants) Act 1975). Implicitly these provisions, in contrast to what is currently available to unmarried cohabitants, redress the respective economic disadvantage and unjust enrichment of weaker and stronger partners suffered as a consequence of the traditional division of labour between married partners. This is why, in most cases where assets exceed needs, an equal division of assets on divorce is made (see *White v White* [2001] 1 AC 596, *Cowan v Cowan* [2001] 2 FLR 192, *Lambert v Lambert* [2002] 3 FCR 673). As we have seen, such a functional approach would find favour with the majority of cohabitants and indeed of the British public at large who cannot understand the need to apply different rules to families who are performing the same role within society.

Would equating the legal effects of unmarried cohabitation with marriage in this way irreparably undermine the institution of marriage? This seems doubtful. It can be argued that legal assimilation of cohabitation would reduce incentives to marry. However, this is unlikely to be the case because, as we have seen, decisions to marry or cohabit are not made in consideration of the legal position. Rather marriage is increasingly taken up for social reasons—to have a 'proper wedding' as performance and display. In addition, even for the few people who do take decisions on such legally rational criteria, the legal advantages of marriage apply particularly to the economically weaker spouse. Thus for the legally rational economically stronger spouse, there would appear to be an equally strong disincentive to marry or at least an incentive to enter into a pre-nuptial agreement ring-fencing their wealth before tying the knot. This attitude has been confirmed in recent press coverage of the high profile divorce of the former Arsenal and England footballer Ray Parlour, whose former wife and mother of his three children was not only awarded a large share of his assets but also a significant share of his future earnings, at least over the next four year period in a landmark Court of Appeal ruling (*Parlour v Parlour* [2004]). This further widens the gulf between the married and unmarried on relationship breakdown (see *The Observer*, 11 July 2004).

7 CONCLUSION

For centuries, marriage has been the epicentre of family law. It must be said that a national system of marriage registration, which clearly and publicly records the ostensibly lifelong commitment made by two married partners to their intimate relationship in a tri-partite contract to which the state itself is the third party, is uniquely able to control the contractual terms in an administratively convenient way. Law—or at least legal policy makers—likes to set *a priori* principles which set standards for society. But in this most personal of spheres surely legal policy makers alone cannot abrogate the power to re-establish married relationships as the only acceptable family structure—even if this were possible. Whereas in the past law has been used in this sphere in a directly interventionist way to set moral standards and stigmatise unmarried relationships and illegitimacy, the appropriateness of such laws was underlined by shared religious and moral values. Today these shared values have gone.

The social structures that gave marriage its power to attract people into, and hold them in, partnerships for life have been greatly weakened. Externally imposed religious and moral codes are a declining force, women's financial and emotional independence has increased, people see partnership more as part of personal fulfilment than a social duty, sex and childbearing are now separated from marriage, and both divorce and cohabitation are accepted and pervasive. Hence, we are currently in a state of transition which is multi-layered and not easy to compartmentalise in the simplistic terms of 'marriage versus cohabitation'. In the face of these changes, law seems a very blunt instrument with which to try to reverse such powerful social forces. Human rights law in any event forbids discrimination against children of unmarried parents (Articles 8 and 14, European Convention on Human Rights, *Marckx v Belgium* (1979) 2 EHRR 330). English law must comply with these principles, making it impossible to return to the old brand of Victorian values even if this were thought politically desirable (see Barlow and James, 2004).

The New Labour government which took power in 1997 has had the opportunity to decide the way forward. Following the previous Conservative administration's fairly disastrous attempts to reassert 'traditional family values' (Fox Harding, 1996), it could have taken up the challenge to modernise family law in England and Wales. Yet instead the New Labour government published *Supporting Families* (Home Office, 1998)—the first ever British family policy document. Far from modernising family law in line with changed social norms and practice, this document promotes marriage and virtually ignores cohabitation. Since 1998, and largely at the instigation of the government's non-discrimination agenda, there has been some shifting of the legal norms—almost in defiance of the government's own rhetoric. As we have seen, new unmarried fathers do now acquire parental responsibility when jointly registering their child's birth with the mother. In addition, after much controversial debate driven by the same-sex equality agenda, the Adoption and Children Act 2002 permits adoption of a child by 'two people (whether of different sexes or the same sex) living as partners in an enduring family relationship' (s144(b)). This is a truly radical step yet to be taken by many jurisdictions which have abolished other legal distinctions between married and cohabiting couples, such as Sweden (Swedish Parents and Children Code 1949, chapter 4, sections 3 and 4). Another government-endorsed change is to the category of people able to register a death which in addition to spouses will include 'life partners' (as yet undefined), if the recommendations of the government White Paper *Civil Registration: Vital Change* (Home Office, 2002) are implemented.

Since commencing our study in 2000, the need for the law governing marriage and cohabitation to respond differently to social change has been endorsed by both the Law Society and the Law Commission. The Law Society has put forward proposals which, alongside the introduction of a civil partnership register for same-sex couples, would broadly assimilate the rights and remedies of unmarried cohabitants with married couples—albeit retaining a superior quality of remedy for married couples (Law Society, 2002). The Law Commission in their discussion paper, on the other hand, found it 'impossible' to reform property law so as to improve the lot of unmarried home-sharers, including cohabitants, but did recommend that the position of cohabitants should be looked at more broadly. It stated:

> We accept that marriage is a status deserving of special treatment. However, we have identified, in the course of this project, a wider need for the law to recognise and to respond to the increasing diversity of living arrangements in this country. We believe that further consideration should be given to the adoption—necessarily by legislation—of broader based approaches to personal relationships, such as the registration of certain civil partnerships and/or the imposition of legal rights and obligations on individuals who are or have been involved in a relationship outside marriage. (Law Commission, 2002: iv)

Seemingly, the issue of how law should respond to changing social norms has become of greater interest to a government which, at the beginning of its first term of office, appeared convinced that a reassertion of marriage alone was best. However, by 2004 its approach was contradictory. In pressing ahead with a Civil Partnership Register limited to same-sex couples, which virtually mirrors marriage in its terms of entry and exit (Civil Partnership Act 2004), the government seems to be more focused on taking the form approach to regulating cohabitation. On the other hand it has not completely abandoned the functional piecemeal approach to law reform, as the changes to fathers' legal rights and adoption law have shown. Rather than continue in this ad hoc way, which only adds to the confusion and contradiction, the next chapter will consider models of more cohesive reform in the light of our own research findings.

6

Reforming the Law: Options for Cohabitation Law

1 INTRODUCTION

There is now a consensus that the legal position of cohabitants is complex and confusing (see Law Commission, 2002; Law Society, 2002), a situation acknowledged to be compounded by the widespread nature of the common law marriage myth (Law Commission, 2002; DTI Women and Equality Unit, 2003a: para 2.8). There is, however, little unanimity as to the question of what, if anything, should be done. This is of course ultimately a policy decision. However it is one, given its potential effect on private and family life in Britain, which should be taken with careful consideration of the reality of *démariage*, as reviewed at length in chapters 2–5. In this chapter, we shall look first at the compelling reasons why our current marriage-centred family law needs to respond to this changed social reality at the turn of the twenty-first century. Secondly, we will try to distil principles appropriate to guiding any legal reform. Finally, we shall evaluate possible models for reform in the context of our research findings, assess current proposals for reform, and examine the experiences of other jurisdictions facing the same challenges.

2 REASONS FOR A LEGAL RESPONSE

The reasons for responding to the situation cohesively, rather than continuing the policy of ignoring cohabitation or responding in an ad hoc way—like current policy (see chapter 5)—are in our view five-fold. First, is the sheer number of people choosing to cohabit for lengthening periods of time as demonstrated in chapter 2. This weakens the case for marriage-centred regulation of families. For, whereas in the past marriage-based family law would apply to almost all families, by the turn of the century increasing numbers of couples are dependent on complex and confusing cohabitation law. This has developed in a piecemeal way and fails, in contrast to the law governing the married, to decide matters on cohesive family law principles. As we have seen in chapter 1, this discriminates against not only the adult partners involved in such relationships, but also their children. As Rebecca Bailey-Harris has asserted: 'the statistics demand a response' (1996:137). This situation is represented diagrammatically in Figure 6.1 below. As the centre of gravity of partnering and parenting moves away from marriage, the fewer the number of couples protected by family law principles specifically designed and developed to regulate the conflicting interests of family members. Thus, arguably, the less appropriate family law protection and regulation of just married couples becomes. The social trend away from marriage into unmarried cohabitation (represented by the increasing visibility of the white circles in Figure 6.1) suggests that, at the very least, a cohesive response of the law to the position of cohabitants is needed.

FIGURE 6.1: *Continuum of Marriage-Centric Regulation*

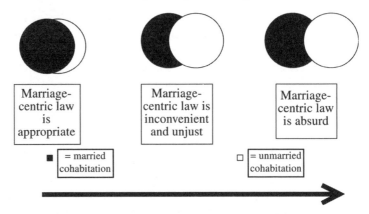

Source: Adapted from Clive, 'Marriage: an Unnecessary Legal Concept', 1980.

A second reason for a cohesive legal response is the common law marriage myth. As chapter 3 has vividly illustrated, some 59 per cent of cohabitants believe they have the same rights as married couples, a view shared by over half of the population at large. Younger people, who are most likely to cohabit, are even more susceptible to the myth. Not to address such a widespread misconception would be to leave large numbers of people stranded in a complex legal jungle with no retrospective remedy at the point at which their legal vulnerability becomes apparent.

A third reason suggesting the need for legal reform is the fact that, as we have seen in the last chapter, the vast majority of people believe that the law *should* treat functionally alike married and cohabiting couples in the same way. This is a view underpinned by the social acceptability of cohabitation as a partnering and parenting structure. People see no reason why a cohabiting couple of some years' standing—with or without children—should not have the same legal safeguards and remedies as a married couple in the same position. There may be reasons why it is seen as both convenient and desirable by law-makers to preserve a difference between married and cohabiting couples in terms of the legal remedies available to them. However, such reasons are not endorsed by either cohabitants themselves or the nationally representative BSA survey respondents. Whilst law-making is not generally directly driven by what people think the law should be, it may be inappropriate in this most personal of spheres to ignore widespread social perceptions of what is just and morally right.

Fourth, as chapter 4 has shown, many cohabitants—whilst they have not made a formal and publicly visible commitment—do express high levels of commitment to their relationship and their family, and demographically similar groups of married and cohabiting partners exhibit similar sorts of behaviour. Conversely, marriage in itself does not guarantee lasting commitment. Even where some cohabitants may be less committed (in the sense that their relationship is more susceptible to breakdown for reasons discussed in chapters 4 and 5), this does not of itself make them less deserving of legal protection when a partner dies or the relationship fails. And even if it did, this argument can hardly apply to their children. The spectrum of cohabitants is broad and it is all too easy to cast them all wrongly as 'less committed' than married couples, and therefore less deserving of legal protection.

Last but not least is the fact that people are not 'legally rational' in the sense which policy makers expect. For the majority, the decision to marry or cohabit is little influenced by the respective legal position of cohabitants and married couples, whatever they believe that position to be, as chapters 3 and 4 have shown. What is more, even when people are aware of their legal vulnerability as cohabitants, few react by making wills, or declarations of home ownership or parental responsibility agreements, as we saw in our discussion in the last two chapters.

For all these reasons, policy makers risk falling into what we have called a 'rationality mistake' (Barlow and Duncan, 2000). They may create policy assuming a particular sort of public behaviour and rationality, whereas in fact most people make their decisions according to different criteria. In this case, policy makers assume that people make decisions in a legally rational way where marriage will be the best option for partnering and parenting, and if people do not choose marriage then they must be either ill-informed (the common law marriage myth) or uncommitted. As chapters 4 and 5 have shown, this is not the case; rather real families (as opposed to the 'virtual families' perceived by current policy) make decisions according to moral, relational and emotional judgements of what is the proper thing to do in their situation. To preserve this rationality mistake, by not reforming cohabitation law, may be to risk a permanent rupture between social and legal norms. This could completely undermine the credibility of the law in relation to families. This, as we shall develop later, would take matters way beyond what Dewar has termed 'the normal chaos of family law' (Dewar, 1998).

3 PRINCIPLES GUIDING REFORM—THE 'FUNCTION VERSUS FORM' DICHOTOMY

In our assessment, the way forward for future family regulation depends on the answer to one key policy question. Should family law continue to favour status or 'form' over 'function and effects' as the principal regulatory rationale? Or, to put this question another way, why does family law privilege the marriage relationship? Why is it regarded as worthy of special legal treatment? Let us consider the possibilities.

Privilege through Contract?

Given that marriage is a tri-partite contract between the spouses and the state based on exclusive and life-long commitment of the spouses to each other, during the marriage (and indeed on death) the contractual legal nexus between the parties is clear. This nexus can then be taken as a guide to the legal treatment of the spouse or surviving spouse in relation to legal procedures assuming that the marriage contract has not been breached by either spouse. This would account for the presumption that a mother's husband is the father of her child and should have parental responsibility. It explains the spousal right to occupy the family home regardless of its legal ownership, the right to register the death of a spouse and the right to inherit their spouse's assets automatically and tax free on death. This contractual reasoning could also be extended to the redistribution of family assets on divorce. One possibility is that the state considers that the law should provide compensation to the 'innocent' party for their loss when the contract is breached or otherwise terminated. This may have been the position in the past when financial provision awards on divorce, like divorce itself, were determined in accordance with the parties' respective innocence or blameworthiness in bringing the marriage to an end (see for example the Matrimonial Causes Act 1937 where maintenance was only payable to a blameless wife for so long as she remained sexually faithful to her ex-husband). Such an approach, punishing the party who had failed to ensure the marriage endured for life and compensating their 'innocent' spouse and other dependants could be seen to be founded on breach of contract principles and could only arise as between the parties to the marriage contract.

This contractual approach is, however, now largely irrelevant for divorce, as this is currently based on the sole and no-fault principle of 'irretrievable breakdown of marriage' (s1 MCA 1973) with fault being a symptom rather than the cause of a divorce situation. Even where fault is alleged, this rarely affects the way in which the family assets are redistributed on divorce, where conduct can only be considered where it would be 'inequitable to disregard it' (s25(2)(g) MCA 1973). This has been interpreted so as to exclude the typical misconduct arising in divorce situations such as adultery or unreasonable behaviour, which will only be taken into account if it is serious or extreme (see for example *K v K (Financial Provision: Conduct)* [1990] 2 FLR 225; Lord Denning in *Wachtel v Wachtel* [1973] Fam 72, moving away from fault-based awards, concluded that the conduct must be 'obvious and gross'). Instead, as we have noted, assets are redistributed having regard to the income and other assets of each party, now and in the future, their current and future needs, obligations and responsibilities, their respective ages, the duration of the marriage and their contribution to the welfare of the family (see s25 MCA 1973). In the latter context 'good' conduct, such as helping to build up a family business, may give rise to a higher award even if, in fact, this happened during a period of pre-marital cohabitation (*Kokosinski v Kokosinski* [1980] Fam 72) and in both *W v W (Judicial Separation: Ancillary Relief)* [1995] 2 FLR 259 and more recently *GW v RW* [2003] EWHC 611 where there had been long periods of pre-marital cohabitation it was the length of the relationships rather than of the marriages themselves that guided the court's awards. In a short marriage where there are no children, the aim is to restore the parties to their pre-marital positions (*Attar v Attar* [1985] FLR 649, *Hobhouse v Hobhouse* [1999] 1 FLR 961) rather than compensate for the early breach of the contract by one party against the wishes of the other. Yet if there is a child born to a short marriage and no pre-marital cohabitation, future needs will enhance the capital sum awarded to the primary carer to compensate for the effect this will have on their ability to earn a living (see eg *C v C (Financial Provision: Short Marriage)* [1997] 2 FLR 26). Similar principles also apply to claims made by spouses under the Inheritance (Provision for Family and Dependants) Act 1975 where a spouse dies without leaving their partner reasonable financial provision in their will. Thus the breach of contract argument for privileging marriage cannot, we suggest, be sustained in the context of no-fault divorce.

Another contract-based rationale explaining financial provision on divorce would be that the parties to the marriage have by the very act of marrying agreed to pool their assets. Marriage, unlike unmarried cohabitation, does impose an enforceable obligation on spouses to maintain each other during marriage (s27 MCA 1973, s1 Domestic Proceedings and Magistrates' Courts Act 1978) and this may be continued on divorce (s23 MCA 1973). However, unlike other European jurisdictions such as France or The Netherlands where a pooling of capital assets known as a 'community of property' is specifically created on marriage and made very clear to the parties, who may if they wish agree to opt out of the regime, in England and Wales we have a system of separate property during marriage. This means that marriage does not affect each spouse's property as no pooling even of assets acquired after marriage is imposed by law and each spouse's assets continue to be owned by that spouse alone (Married Women's Property Act 1882). This remains the case unless they divorce or one of them dies, at which point, as we have seen, assets may be redistributed in accordance with state-imposed statutory criteria (s25 MCA 1973, s46 Administration of Estates Act 1925, Inheritance (Provision for Dependants) Act 1975) rather than any explicit pre-marital consent to redistribution in the event of divorce or death. Pre-marital (or pre-nuptial) agreements avoiding the statutory criteria (and which are arguably evidence that there is no such implied consent) are not guaranteed success. Whilst the courts have recently been more willing to take these into account (see for example *K v K (Ancillary Relief: Prenuptial Agreement)* [2003]1 FLR 120 and *M v M (Prenuptial Agreement)* [2002] FL 177), they are not specifically enforceable and cannot override the court's jurisdiction to make appropriate financial provision on divorce (see *Uddin v Ahmed* [2001] 3 FCR 300).

Thus it is something other than legal contractual principles which is guiding the law of financial provision on divorce. Breaches of the contract are not directly or consistently compensated under our family law, and the parties are unable to avoid the state-imposed rules governing asset redistribution on divorce by entering into a pre-marital contract to which they each give specific and informed consent. Rather family law's protective function overrides any contractual principles. At best, it can be argued that marriage implies a general and uninformed consent to redistribution of assets on divorce or death in accordance with statutory criteria which may change over time and in which the needs and non-financial contributions of the economically weaker spouse may take priority over the financial contributions of their partner. However, the reality is that these terms are in fact imposed at the point of divorce (or in some cases death) rather than an understood feature of the marriage contract at its inception. We therefore continue our search for a clearer reason as to why the law metes out special treatment to married partners in the absence of specific contractual consent.

Rewarding Special Commitment in Marriage?

Is the rationale for privileging marriage embodied in the 'special commitment involved in marriage' to which legislation and case law sometimes refer (see s41 Family Law Act 1996 and *Midland Bank v Cooke* [1995] 4 All ER 562)? Mutually committed relationships are seen as superior to contingently committed relationships (see chapter 4) in that they are more stable, last longer and involve the parties working as a team for a common purpose—certainly they are more appropriate for raising children who thrive on stability and (other than in violent or abusive relationships) from knowing both parents (see Morgan, 2000). This precept links into a general assumption by family law that the best, or at least the most visible, indicator of mutual commitment is where the parties are married, for the parties are publicly committing themselves to each other in principle for life. This style of commitment is cast as 'special' in family law. It is also, given this reasoning, easy to identify. We have a reliable system of marriage registration, which will show whether and when a couple are married in this jurisdiction. There are also rules governing recognition of foreign marriages which can take account of a spectrum of cultural differences alongside Caribbean beach weddings currently fashionable with British nationals, and mean that the production of a marriage certificate will usually be conclusive proof of an assumed high quality commitment which began on a fixed date. Clearly, from the state's point of view, marriage is a convenient test of commitment. Yet is it a test which is genuinely and appropriately sorting out committed from uncommitted relationships, and how relevant is this assumed 'special' commitment to the award of legal remedies anyway?

We would suggest that the high divorce rate in Britain alone makes marriage an imperfect and inadequate test of the quality of commitment given in a relationship and makes the commitment given in marriage less 'special' than it used to be from a regulatory point of view. Marriage does not of itself guarantee high quality commitment and family law-style regulation of married couples alone leaves similar quality commitment given in unmarried relationships unrecognised and unrewarded. If it is relationship commitment (rather than just being married) which the law seeks to encourage and reward, the increasing number and duration of cohabitation relationships (chapter 2) alone throws doubt on the unique character of marital commitment and therefore on the suitability of marriage as the sole or principal trigger for family law privilege. Furthermore the high levels of commitment expressed in our follow-up study by cohabitants to their partners and their relationships adds to existing evidence (eg Lewis, 2001) of high quality commitment in many cohabiting relationships, with demographically similar groups of married and cohabiting partners tending to exhibit similar sorts of behaviour (see chapter 4). The law itself has recognised this problem to a degree, treating cohabitants as married for tax credit and many welfare benefit purposes and extending remedies (albeit sometimes of an inferior nature) to marriage-like cohabitants in certain situations, including now adoption of a child (s144 Adoption and Children Act 2002).

In terms of whether the commitment given in marriage—cast in family law as 'special'—is a credible justification for the continued privileging of marriage, one cannot escape the irony that this public declaration of life-long commitment to a marriage is now mainly rewarded in the event of divorce. Indeed the ease of divorce has perhaps unwittingly devalued the nature of the commitment involved in marriage, which surely in today's reality is contingent—it amounts to little more than a public promise to stay together unless or until one or other of the partners wishes to end the relationship. Indeed, as we discussed in chapter 4, modern marriage—where commitment is no longer understood as unconditional—needs easy divorce if it is to continue for the majority. The fact that marriage provides a convenient measure of high level commitment to the relationship is probably one reason why marriage is privileged in family law. However, it does not explain why other cohabiting relationships which demonstrate a similar quality of commitment are still treated as inferior. What other factors are influencing the current approach?

Remoralising the Family?

Perhaps, then, using marriage as a measure of commitment is part of a grander plan to use legal incentives to 'remoralise' the family by promoting marriage. This is a key policy in the USA (see Bowman, 2004). In Britain government rhetoric has promoted marriage as the main forum for raising children (Home Office, 1998). As discussed in chapter 5, seems neither sensible nor possible. In addition, the legal incentives currently provided are by their very nature double-edged. Pension rights and Inheritance Tax exemptions for (home-owning) spouses may provide a good reason to marry (were people to adopt legally rational thinking), but on divorce the financial 'reward' for this superior married commitment is given only to the weaker economic spouse regardless of their role in the breakdown of the marriage. This ironically leaves a 'bread-winning' and 'innocent' spouse suffering an indisputable 'commitment penalty' which, if people were to act in accordance with legal rationality, would provide the richer partner with a perverse incentive not to marry.

Equally troubling is the fact that choosing other styles of more private commitment is deemed inferior and consequently penalised. One poignant example is provided in the context of applications for occupation orders (usually sought in domestic violence situations) by 'non-entitled' cohabitants (that is, those who do not own or rent the family home in their name). Here, at least until the Domestic Violence Crime and Victims Act 2004 is implemented, the court must take account of the fact that the parties have not given each other 'the commitment involved in marriage' (s36 and s41 Family Law Act 1996). The assumed superior nature of married commitment may then mean that a cohabitant is less likely to successfully exclude a violent partner from the family home than their married counterpart in the same situation. What sort of marriage could this be aimed at promoting?

Thus whilst marriage is used—incorrectly we would argue—as a shorthand measure for commitment in many family law contexts, it is not even used consistently either to reward such commitment or to promote marriage. Perhaps a greater consistency emerges if the regulatory rationale is seen to be driven by a need to balance the functions and effects of the married relationship on each of the parties to the marriage at the point when it becomes necessary for the law to intervene—most commonly on divorce or on the death of a spouse. Let us consider whether this is the case.

Function and Effects of the Marriage Relationship

Both family legislation and case law developed by the courts have in recent years been mindful of the way in which marriage (particularly as a site for parenting) performs a useful function for society but may commonly distort the parties' respective economic positions. This, it has been accepted, needs to be redressed on divorce irrespective, in all but the most extreme cases, of why the marriage broke down.

Thus in the process of modernising marriage through permitting no-fault divorce after just one year of marriage (s3 MCA 1973), the underlying justifications for asset redistribution on divorce and death have become related principally to the functions and effects of marriage, rather than to its agreed contractual terms or its style of commitment—as the following examples will now demonstrate.

First, the significance of the parties' conduct as one factor set out in the s25 MCA 1973 criteria which guide the court's redistribution of assets on divorce has been minimised. In addition, other 1984 amendments to s25 acknowledged that it was impossible to achieve the section's original guiding principle 'to place the parties as nearly as possible in the position they would have been in if the marriage had not broken down' (Matrimonial and Family Proceedings Act 1984). Instead, the court has a duty to consider whether it is appropriate to impose a 'clean break'—that is, terminate the parties' financial obligations to each other as soon after the grant of the decree as the court considers just and reasonable (s25A MCA 1973). This in the past has been used to increase the capital assets transferred to (typically) the wife in return for no maintenance payments. However, this may be less appropriate or indeed possible where there are children of the family in relation to whom Child Support payments must be made (Child Support Act 1991). Whilst no new overall guiding principle was inserted in the amended 1973 legislation, the courts as discussed in chapter 1 can be seen to have interpreted the amended s25 and s25A so as to prioritise the interests of the children and most recently to equalise the value between financial contributions to the family (typically made mainly by men) and non-financial contributions to the family (typically credited mainly to women) (see *White v White* [2001] AC 596, *Lambert v Lambert* [2003] EWCA Civ 1685).

Second is the prime consideration now given to children. Section 25 (in contrast to the provisions available to separating cohabiting parents) does require the court on making financial provision orders on divorce to 'have regard to all the circumstances of the case, first consideration being given to the welfare, while a minor of any child of the family'. Whilst the child's interests are just the first and not the paramount consideration, this has been broadly interpreted to ensure that by dividing up the pool of assets belonging to both parties, the children of the family have a stable home combined with stable continuity of care. This should provide both parties with sufficient funds to enable new family homes to be purchased for each party but often involves allowing the primary carer spouse to continue to live in the home with the children (see eg *B v B (Financial Provision: Welfare of Child and Conduct)* [2002] 1 FLR 555, *Cordle v Cordle* [2002] 1 FCR 97, *M v B (Ancillary Relief)* [1998] 1 FLR 53 approved in *Piglowska v Piglowski* [1999] 2 FLR 763 HL). Either of these results can normally only be achieved by a significant redistribution of (and/or deferral of access to) family assets in accordance with the other criteria set out in s25 MCA 1973. These include the standard of living during the marriage, the age of the parties and duration of the marriage, the parties' respective current and future income and assets, needs and resources as well as financial and (critically) non-financial contributions made and likely to be made to the welfare of the family by each of the parties.

Third, case law has recently come to interpret the s25 criteria to require the economically stronger spouse to compensate the economically weaker spouse (usually the primary carer of the children and typically the wife) for their non-financial contributions to the welfare of the family so as to enable them to adjust to their new situation. Significantly, contributions to the welfare of the family during long term premarital cohabitation will also be taken into account even (or perhaps especially) where the marriage has been short (*W v W (Judicial Separation: Ancillary Relief)* [1995] 2 FLR 259, *GW v RW* [2003] EWHC 611). This underlines the view that it is the effects of marriage-like relationships on the parties' respective positions that are being compensated or rewarded, rather than the terms of the marriage contract itself. At least where there has been a long marriage and assets exceed needs, the perceived value of such non-financial contributions by the courts has greatly increased, permitting an equal split of the assets and even a large share of future earning capacity at least for a limited period of time post divorce (see *Lambert v Lambert* [2003] EWCA Civ 1685, *McFarlane v McFarlane* and *Parlour v Parlour* [2004] EWCA Civ 872). These developments have taken place notwithstanding the fact that women today are generally far more able to be financially independent than in the past. Thus at least where assets are plentiful and the marriage long, the financial provision made on divorce is no longer driven by and limited to the weaker economic spouse's needs or reasonable requirements (see *Dart v Dart* [1996] 2 FLR 286). The system has moved from a welfare-based redistribution to an entitlement-based redistribution (Eekelaar, 2001), which has conceded equality between financial and non-financial contributions to the welfare of the family in line with some but not other strands of feminist thought (Fineman, 1991, cf Deech, 1980). In cases where the relationship between assets and needs is inverted or more finely balanced, it is the needs of the children and thus of the primary carer that will shape the settlement, often ensuring that the economically weaker wife will take over half the assets. Implicitly these provisions redress the economic disadvantage and unjust enrichment where they are suffered as a consequence of the traditional division of labour between partners in a married relationship and recognise the poorer labour market position of women as compared with men and particularly those whose earning capacity is or has been disadvantaged by undertaking the bulk of a family's childcare. As Hale J (as she then was) explained in the Court of Appeal in *SRJ v DWJ (Financial Provision)* [1999] 2 FLR 179 at 182:

> It is not only in [the child's] interests but in the community's interests that parents, whether mothers or fathers and spouses, whether husbands or wives, should have a real choice between concentrating on breadwinning and concentrating on home-making and child-rearing, and do not feel forced, for fear of what might happen should their marriage break down much later in

life, to abandon looking after the home and the family to other people for the sake of maintaining a career.

Whether or not this approach is appropriate in the married context is a matter of live debate (Parker, 1998; Bailey-Harris, 2001; Fineman, 1991; Carbone and Brinig, 1991), but in practice it has served to widen the gulf between the remedies available to 'as good as married' cohabitants as compared with married couples on relationship breakdown or death. This reduces the post-relationship standard of living of both the weaker economic cohabitant and any children of the relationship living with them.

Thus we can see that it is the function and effects of marriage and the best interests of children that have prompted family law to enhance the protection offered to the weaker economic spouse and primary carer on divorce or death of their partner—the marital contract and assumed commitment given in marriage only add to this rationale for legally privileging marriage. The overriding justification for this approach therefore relates to what families do, rather than the form they take. But if this is the case, then on what grounds can these legal privileges be restricted to married couples?

Can we Justify Privileging Marriage Alone?

Given that we have seen that the function and effects of marriage and long term cohabitation are broadly the same, the justification for privileging marriage above other functionally similar families would either rest on the Napoleonic adage that cohabitants 'ignore the law and so the law ignores them' or result from a belief in the innate superiority of this family form. If the state considers that marriage is best and takes the view that the role of law is to establish *a priori* principles according to which society's standards are set, including its personal moral standards (Deech, 1980), then a form-based approach which promotes marriage would have a clear rationale. This approach would also command some support from religious organisations and other social commentators who regard marriage as innately superior (Morgan, 2000; Phillips, 2001). But as discussed above, and as we examined in detail in chapters 4 and 5, this assumption of the innate superiority of marriage for partnering and parenting does not hold in social terms. Even if it did, large numbers of people do not partner and parent in this way and so enforcing marriage would either not work, or would work through oppression, and would certainly bring the law into public contempt. We are left, then, with the 'Napoleonic' explanation. From the point of view of the state, marriage is an administratively convenient way of regulating families. But, as the numbers choosing to partner and parent within marriage lessen, this approach leaves growing numbers of people outside family law's cohesive protective and regulatory framework. (At this point is family law not missing its target?) Even the Napoleonic reason for privileging marriage crumbles.

What is more, any policy strongly favouring a form approach to family law, in order to promote marriage, may not avoid unlawfully discriminating against children of unmarried families (Human Rights Act 1998, *Marcx v Belgium* (1979) 2 EHRR 330). In time, given that the European Convention on Human Rights is accepted to be a 'living instrument' responsive to social change within Europe, indirect discrimination against children of unmarried cohabitants who have fewer rights on relationship breakdown might even be considered to be in breach of its non-discrimination provision (Article 14 ECHR). This provision has already been used successfully to reduce discrimination against same-sex couples in the domestic courts (eg *Ghaidan v Godin-Mendoza* [2004] UKHL 30 and see Barlow and James, 2004). The Napoleonic policy of ignoring cohabitants may well be equally unsustainable in the longer term.

Bearing all this in mind, policy makers could decide that a function-based reform might better meet the aims of family law in the 21st century. In the next section we will examine some possible models for reform.

4 OPTIONS FOR REFORM

Let us now evaluate the relative merits of the options for reform open to policy makers and legislators in the context of both our research findings, and the experiences of reforms in other jurisdictions. In making this assessment we are mindful of the criticism made by some (Deech, 1990; cf Eekelaar and Maclean, 1990; O'Donovan, 1993) that family law reform (at least in the divorce context) has been over-reliant on small-scale empirical studies which predicate proposals for reform on what prove to be inaccurately predicted social responses, instead of rationally established *a priori* principles. In order to avoid any such pitfalls, our study uses a combination of both extensive research based on a nationally representative sample and in-depth intensive research based on a broad range of qualitative interviews (see chapter 1 and Appendix 2). This study is combined with a review of other research in the area. Our findings suggest that a pluralistic legal and policy response is needed to accommodate the growing diversity of families. In this way our preferred model for reform aims to strike a balance between the need for individual autonomy, perhaps best served by private ordering, and the need to apply the protective function of family law to address an axiomatic exploitation by the powerful of the less powerful within family relationships (Barlow and James, 2004). The aim of such reform would be to remove the confusion and complexity surrounding the rights of cohabitants, remove any perverse incentives not to marry and as far as possible ensure that the principal aims of family law—often categorised as protective, adjustive and supportive (Eekelaar, 1984)—are applied to all cohabiting families in a cohesive way.

If we accept the premise that family law-based reform (as opposed to say property-based reform) is needed, as established earlier in the book and as argued by the Law Society (2002), the Law Commission (2002), and the Solicitors' Family Law Association (2000), then options for reform can be broken down into two main groups. The first possibility would be to adopt a stronger status or form approach, which would make clear that legal rights only accrue on gaining a particular status in the manner prescribed by law. This need not be limited to marriage and could be extended to cohabiting partners (same sex and/or different sex) who gain a new status on registration of their relationship which need not be modelled on marriage. The second possibility would be to start from the premise that families which are alike should be regulated alike, that is, in a manner appropriate to their function and irrespective of their form. However, to avoid oppression of those who genuinely wish to avoid marriage-like regulation, reform would also need to acknowledge that 'one size does not fit all' and provide a legal framework which offers both protection and choice for different styles of family. This could be done by permitting cohabitants to agree to opt out of a default function-based legislation. These two approaches are now considered in turn.

The Extended-Form Approach—Marriage plus Civil Partnership Register plus Public Information Campaign

As we have seen, to regulate according to form or status is an administratively convenient approach. This approach combines well with a marriage promotion agenda (which deliberately privileges marriage), but there is no reason why this could not be extended to other family forms endorsed by the state, for example through registered civil partnerships. It leaves those who do not marry or register their partnership free from any automatically imposed marriage-like regulation and free instead to undertake, or not, private ordering of their own choosing. It is therefore an approach which can encourage, protect and privilege marriage, extend these legal protections to registering cohabitants, and safeguard the autonomy of those choosing not to marry. This new situation could be backed up by a public information campaign aimed at unmarried and unregistered cohabitants to counteract the common law marriage myth. It is therefore at first sight a very attractive option which also has the allure of simplicity.

However, this 'extended-form' approach has one crucial problem—it implicitly assumes that law can shape social change. It is built on the premise that if law privileges marriage and registered partnerships strongly enough, and denies equivalent family law rights and protection to unmarried or unregistered cohabitants, then people, provided they are aware of the situation, will respond by marrying (or registering) in greater numbers. This will, in turn, restore formal marriage alongside registered partnerships as a social norm.

Our findings suggest that this approach is flawed because of its assumption that people are legally rational in this sense. The majority do not choose to marry or cohabit because of the legal consequences. This may be because many are unaware of the legal consequences, believing instead in the existence of common law marriage. But as we have seen (chapters 4 and 5), even when partners are aware of the legal distinctions, this is hardly ever the basis upon which the decision to marry or cohabit is made. Nor does this all-important knowledge prompt any wide-scale appropriate private ordering, often despite intentions to take the necessary legal steps. We are therefore pessimistic as to the likelihood of success of this extended-form plus public information approach and our pessimism is fortified by related research as part of the Scottish Social Attitudes Survey (Barlow, 2002). In Scotland, although there are proposals for reform (Scottish Executive, 2000), the law, in contrast to that in England and Wales, has made very few concessions to cohabitants. Marriage remains the only form of family relationship recognised for the purpose of family law rights and protection on relationship breakdown or death, with not even any inferior marriage-like remedies available to cohabitants as in England and Wales. Nonetheless, despite the lack of legal protection available, the 2000 Scottish Social Attitudes Survey survey found that very similar proportions of people were cohabiting in Scotland (31 per cent) as compared with England and Wales (35 per cent in the BSA survey). Whilst an old form of common law marriage, 'marriage by cohabitation, habit and repute' is still recognised in Scotland, this affects very few cohabiting couples. For in order to establish such a marriage, cohabitants must both publicly hold themselves out as married and establish a legal proof that this is publicly accepted—which the vast majority do not (Bissett-Johnson and Barton, 1999). Furthermore, social attitudes towards marriage in Scotland were no different, with cohabitation being fully accepted as a partnering and parenting structure. Most significantly, in terms of legal awareness, the number of people who believed that cohabitation automatically gave rise to marriage-like rights was as high as it was in England and Wales (57 per cent) with no or no statistically significant increase in the number of Scottish cohabitants who had made wills (16 per cent), entered parental rights and responsibility agreements (5 per cent) or made declarations as to ownership of a shared home (6 per cent). All this suggests that family law does not hold the power to alter behaviour around cohabitation and marriage in the face of changed social norms.

It is true that neither Scotland nor England and Wales has yet been subject to a sustained public information campaign, although an initiative commissioned by the Department for Constitutional Affairs was begun in England in summer 2004. Citing the BSA survey as revealing a problem to be addressed—but not accepting that the Civil Partnerships Register proposed for same-sex couples should be extended to different-sex couples—the expressed view of the Women and Equality Unit (located in the Department of Trade and Industry and initially charged with considering these issues) seems to be that raising awareness will solve the problem. They state:

> We ... recognise that some unmarried opposite-sex couples are under the mistaken impression that they already have a legally recognised status as 'common law husband and wife'. This misconception can lead to difficulties

...The DCA is leading a cross-government working group to consider how best to raise awareness about the rights and responsibilities of cohabitants and to dispel the myth surrounding 'common law marriage' (DTI, 2003b: para 3.6).

At least from government's perspective, such a campaign will permit the continued privileging of marriage alongside registered partnerships mirroring marriage for same-sex couples. A marriage-model Civil Partnership Register neatly avoids any potentially unlawful discrimination on the grounds of sexual orientation whilst the public information campaign allows them not to address the wider problem of unmarried and unregistered cohabitation. For if government consider that they have done all they can to inform people of their disadvantaged legal situation, this in their view may well justify a return to the Napoleonic approach that the law is entitled to ignore those who ignore it, leaving those who 'choose' not to marry or register with their own unprotected autonomy.

There are two problems with this model for reform. First, it does nothing to prevent the exploitation of less knowledgeable, economically weaker cohabitants (and indirectly their children) by their more knowledgeable partners despite the fact that the legal disincentives to marriage (or registration) for the financially stronger make this very important. For who, given the current law on financial provision on relationship breakdown, would recommend marriage to say a wealthy man who can gain all the advantages of a home maker and child carer partner traditionally associated with marriage through cohabitation, without the risks to his/her assets posed by divorce? The role of family law in protecting economically weaker family members from such exploitation under this option is limited in the main to those who marry or register. The only wider protection envisaged on this model is that the 'rational,' more vulnerable cohabitant will discover the weakness of their unmarried/unregistered position before they have suffered any disadvantage on account of the relationship and then leave their partner if they refuse to marry them/register the partnership. If they don't, then they only have themselves to blame for not acting 'rationally' and must suffer the consequences. This does not seem to be an option which will extend protection to weaker parties or to their children.

Secondly, our research findings tend to suggest that raising awareness will in practice achieve little in terms of persuading people to marry or organise the rather complex private ordering which cohabitation law currently requires. By and large we have found that people do not take decisions according to legal incentives and for policy makers to assume that this is easily changed may be merely to fall prey once again to the rationality mistake (see above and chapter 5).

Despite our pessimism as to how many will respond, some people will undoubtedly be stirred by a publicity campaign into contemplating legal advice to arrange the effects of their cohabitation relationship better. For some cohabitants, this may take the form of a pragmatic decision to marry, as happened in Philip's case (a plumber and JP about to marry his partner: see chapter 3), although other cohabiting interviewees such as Duncan, the Bedford school teacher (see chapter 4) were unhappy about founding a marriage on such a basis. Rather, our study found great public support for a French-style civil partnership register which provides a real alternative to marriage *and* which is open to same and different-sex cohabitants (see chapter 5). This does not, however, accord very well with the government's current (2004) intention to introduce a marriage-mirror civil partnership register limited to same-sex cohabitants (DTI, 2003a; Civil Partnerships Act 2004).

Nonetheless, despite the government's current policy let us stay within our discussion of the extended form-based model for reform, and consider how effective different styles of Registered Civil Partnerships might be in regulating different-sex cohabitants.

Civil Partnership Registers—Progress or Panacea?

Civil Partnership Registers are now common in Europe but may take different forms. There are two main models within which can be found some significant differences in style. The first model extends rights mirroring marriage to same-sex couples only, and it is this group that Britain proposes to join. The second extends rights (which are not necessarily carbon copies of those available to married couples) to both same-sex and different-sex cohabitants.

Same-Sex only Models

Denmark led the way with the first model introducing a Registered Partnership Act in 1989 which essentially extends the legal consequences of marriage to registered partners. This was followed in Norway in 1993, Sweden in 1994, Iceland in 1996 and, most recently, Finland and Germany in 2001 (although in Sweden and Norway the register is complemented by other measures which take them into the 'functional approach' as discussed below). This model mirrors marriage in terms of conditions for entry and the rights and obligations it bestows, save in some jurisdictions rights relating to joint custody and adoption of children and exit from the partnership are achieved by notice rather than divorce (see Barlow, 2004). It is now this marriage-mirror same-sex only model that England and Wales intends to follow in the Civil Partnership Act 2004 currently awaiting implementation, having rejected attempts to introduce registered partnerships for both same and different-sex cohabitants not so directly modelled on marriage (the Relationships (Civil Registration) Bill 2001 introduced to the House of Commons by Jane Griffiths MP, and the Civil Partnerships Bill 2001 introduced into the House of Lords by Lord Lester). The form chosen is clearly intended to end discrimination against same-sex cohabitants who are unable to marry (s11c

MCA 1973), but offers little to different-sex cohabitants who can marry. Indeed, it is even more marriage-like than other European models in that exit is by means of a divorce-like procedure on the simplified grounds of separation and behaviour (although not adultery) and there are no substantive restrictions relating to children. Extending civil partnerships to different-sex alongside same-sex couples was rejected by the British government on the basis that different-sex couples, unlike same-sex couples, have the option to marry if they so wish (DTI, 2003a). Given the very marriage-like nature of the government's Civil Partnership Act, this is a claim that can be made. However, the exclusion of different-sex cohabitants remains controversial as it would at least offer protection to those ideologically opposed to marriage but seeking to publicly demonstrate their commitment. Clumsy amendments introduced in the House of Lords to extend the Bill's terms to different-sex couples and other home-sharers were abandoned and the government's optimism that the Bill would be passed before the end of the Parlimentary session proved well founded (*The Guardian*, 13 October 2004).

Same-Sex and Different-Sex Models

Some other European jurisdictions, notably the Netherlands, some Spanish autonomous regions, France and Belgium, see no problem in civil partnership legislation for both same-and different-sex cohabitants. The Dutch model (which is to be reviewed in 2006) currently allows both same- and different-sex couples to marry and enter into a marriage-mirror model civil partnership and has seen far more registrations by different-sex couples than same-sex couples (http://www.cbs.nl and Boele-Woelki, 2003: 51 who argues that this may be due to the easier exit provisions). The Spanish schemes, unlike that of the Netherlands, are not all exclusively 'form-based' opt-in civil partnership registers but also operate a parallel functional approach to confer marriage-like rights on cohabitants automatically in some situations (Casals, 2003). This will be discussed further below.

However, it is the looser and more flexible commitment embodied in the French and Belgian models that may well prove the most attractive form-based option for different-sex cohabitants, as these do provide a real alternative status to marriage. The French *Pacte Civil de Solidarité* (*PaCS*) Law (Act no 99–944 of 15 November 1999 amending the French Civil Code) introduces the concept of a civil union pact which a cohabiting couple, whether same- or different-sex, may register to regulate their relationship. It defines cohabitation (for the purpose of this and other laws regulating it) without reference to marriage as 'a de facto union characterised by a communal life which demonstrates stability and continuity, between two persons of the same or different-sex, who live as a couple' (Article 3, inserting art 5615–8 into the French Civil Code). Rather than prescribe what happens when the relationship breaks down or one partner dies, the law expects the registered partners to agree the division of their assets (subject to French succession law) and in default of a specific agreement joint ownership of all post-relationship assets is presumed in the same way as it is in French marriage law (community of property). A 'PaCS' couple are recognised as a unit for most tax, insurance and social security purposes in France, gaining marriage-like rights by way of registration of a cohabitation agreement in return for a lesser commitment than that given in marriage and which is terminable on two months' notice. The Belgian Law Establishing Legal Cohabitation 1998 broadly operates in the same way but unlike the French legislation also provides for limited maintenance to be paid on termination of the relationship (see Probert and Barlow, 2000; Barlow, 2004).

This model has not been seriously considered in England and Wales by those advocating a civil partnerships register, partly because it would not fulfil the need to provide a marriage-equivalent for same-sex couples and, perhaps, because it risks proving more popular than marriage. Yet the results of our in-depth interviews reveal that a French-style civil partnership was seen as an attractive option, which might meet the needs of cohabitants not wishing to marry, yet not seeking to avoid commitment. All our interviewees were asked the following question:

> In some countries couples who live together can sign a legal agreement which is filed at a local Court and this agreement sets out certain rights and responsibilities that they've agreed to, in relation to the property, for example. This can be terminated by notice and if they sign the agreement they get similar Social Security and inheritance tax advantages as married couples— what do you think about that idea?

Some such as Eileen, cohabiting for over two years, working as a cleaner and twice married before, thought this was too marriage-like—

> To me signing a piece of paper is the same thing, isn't it, as getting married?

Angela, in her cohabiting relationship for 13 years with one 12 year old son, on the other hand felt it was inferior, not marriage-like enough:

> [It's] being classed as a second-class citizen.

However, over two thirds of our interviewees liked the idea and thought it had potential. Colin, 44 and in his second cohabitation relationship, thought it would avoid argument:

> If someone splits up after like, two years, three years, you've got a legal document there and as I say, it saves all the hassle of going through solicitors and the courts and all that lot. 'Cos you've already got that document there saying that that's what you've signed, that's what you agreed to.

Caroline, who was 22 with two children and had been cohabiting for five years, recognised its usefulness where cohabitation is extended and any intended wedding delayed:

> Yes, definitely because you can meet somebody and you might not get married for 10 or 20 years and something like that, I think it would be quite good to bring something like that in.

We found that those who were most enthusiastic tended to have been married or cohabited in the past. Colin provides a good example of this view:

> Brilliant idea—can they also update it as well? …You know as years go by you can update it—but yes I think that's an excellent idea … Yes, it would appeal to me because like when I go into my next relationship I really will have to have my eyes wide open …

Drawbacks to this model were also identified. Some, such as Gail (a 28 year old nursery nurse, with one child and cohabiting for eight years) who was an enthusiast, recognised that it might prove more attractive than marriage:

> It might put people off getting married—they wouldn't need to get married if they had that already …

If this option were pursued, further consideration of enforceable pre-nuptial agreements for the married ought also to be examined, to tackle the issue of whether partnership registration might become a more popular option than marriage.

Others like Claire, who was 23, had cohabited for six months and had one child, thought that such agreements could be open to abuse:

> I would say that the only problems I would see is people that do it without really thinking about doing it or maybe a partner persuading another partner to do it for other reasons.

Emily did not think it would be a satisfactory substitute for her wish to marry or her partner's reluctance to commit his assets to their joint enterprise:

> No. To me, I want to get married. [My partner] wouldn't have that anyway because he feels what's his is his. I think from his past experiences he's very selfish.

Some also identified the most worrying problem that cohabitants would not actually get around to registering a partnership, but just continue to live day to day. As Jack, who was 32, had cohabited in this relationship for two years and had no children, explained:

> ... you'd have to really force people into thinking about the situation other-
> wise there's a million and one things to think about these days, you just
> wouldn't think about the legal implications.

Naomi, a cohabitant of 15 years, was also realistic:

> I don't know really. If that was brought in would I get round to signing it? I
> know now that I'm in a position where I really ought to sort something out
> legally but I haven't.

If an extended-form approach as discussed earlier was to be the regulatory rationale, a marriage-mirror model civil partnership register as contained in the Civil
Partnership Act 2004 would do little for different-sex cohabitants who did not
want to commit to marriage and amount for them only to a panacea. In contrast,
a PaCS-style model—which as Rebecca Probert has noted is arguably contractual marriage (Probert, 2001)—would offer that group of cohabitants a real choice
as to the style of commitment they wished to give each other. By providing a new
recognised status of coupledom through one simply-registered agreement, it
would also avoid the legal complexity that currently prevails of having to undertake a range of legal measures. Whilst earlier research found that cohabitation
contracts and pre-nuptial agreements were considered too cold, too inflexible and
too American (Lewis, 1999), few of our interviewees felt that such an idea was a
complete anathema to them and it was perceived overall as a useful tool for
cohabitants which would, for them, constitute legal progress.

Thus some aspects of the extended form-based approach are attractive in
allowing both protection and autonomy, but the fundamental problem of leaving
large numbers of cohabitants unprotected by family law from the acknowledged
risks of the functions and effects of family life remains. In particular, this
approach can do nothing to prevent exploitation in the situation where one partner refuses to marry or register. Let us now consider what a more functional
approach to family regulation, as taken up in some regions of Spain, Canada and
Australia, might have to offer, how much social support it might have, and
whether it could be usefully combined with existing or proposed form-based
approaches. In short, can we find a pluralistic response more appropriate to the
plurality of family forms we now find within our society?

A Functional Approach—Equalisation of Rights plus Registered Civil Partnership Opt-out and Information

As we demonstrated above, better legal information and a Civil Partnership
Register on their own would still leave many cohabitants and often their children
disadvantaged. Another option is to equalise the rights of married couples and
long term cohabitants, subject to the possibility of opting out. A key reason for
taking this paternalistic position, rather than a freedom of choice approach, is that

the likely financial detriment—which we know is unequally borne in family relationships—cannot be accurately predicted in advance. As Baroness Hale has succinctly summarised:

> Intimate domestic relationships frequently bring with them inequalities, especially if there are children. They compromise the parties' respective economic positions, often irreparably. This inequality is sometimes compounded by domestic ill-treatment. These detriments cannot be predicted in advance, so there should be remedies that cater for the needs of the situation when it arises. They arise from the very nature of intimate relationships, so it is the relationship rather than the status that should matter. (Hale, 2004: 421)

Such a 'functional' approach has worked successfully in Australia where it now extends beyond cohabitants and married couples to other 'domestic relationships' in some states (eg, New South Wales and Australian Capital Territory). This seems to be an uncontroversial tool designed to adapt the protective aims of family law to serve new needs engendered by social change and new-style living arrangements. Similarly, in Canada, the law has over a number of years assumed parity between the obligations and benefits of spouses and cohabitants (see for example the Modernization of Benefits and Obligations Act, SC 2000, c.12), although recently the Canadian Supreme Court confirmed that it was not unconstitutionally discriminatory for Provincial legislatures to discriminate against unmarried couples in terms of marital property laws (*Attorney General of Nova Scotia v Walsh* (2002) 4 SCR 325, and see Bailey, 2004).

Another useful model for reform can be found in the Spanish autonomous regions (which have responsibility for family and succession law) such as Aragon, Catalonia, Navarra and the Balearic Islands. These jurisdictions, as noted in the last section, have introduced marriage-model Civil Partnership Registers, whose legal protections may also be of benefit to the unregistered. The legislation which introduced the Partnership Registers also operates in the case of different-sex couples (and in some regions also for same-sex couples) to confer marriage-like rights automatically after a period of two or three years of cohabitation or the birth of a child which can be proven 'by any means of proof admitted in law' (Aragon Unmarried Couples Law 1999 article 3, Catalonia Stable Union of De Facto Couples Law 1998 article 2, Navarra Unmarried Stable Couples Law 2000 article 2.2, Balearic Islands Stable Couples Law 2001 article 2.1, and see generally Casals, 2003). This provides a legal remedy to cohabitants whose partners deliberately avoid marriage or registration for their own gain. Sweden and Norway have also extended to different-sex cohabitants the same, or similar, remedies available to married couples alongside their partnership registers. Sweden has taken the most functional approach, based on social needs, to both same- and different-sex cohabitation (Ytterburg, 2001: 430; Agell, 2003: 126). Its

1987 legislation (Cohabitees (Joint Homes) Act and Homosexual Cohabitees Act 1987) recognised that both different- and same-sex cohabitants faced the same problems as married couples when relationships broke down and gives marriage-like rights to cohabitants in relationships 'reminiscent of marriage' (s1). This is judged in accordance with the length of time the couple have been together, whether there are children of the relationship, and whether they have shared daily housekeeping expenses. Norway introduced a Joint Households Act in 2002 which deals with cohabitants of two or more years' standing or who have or are expecting a child together but is not restricted to sexual relationships. It does not provide for the sharing of the value of jointly used assets as in Sweden but merely governs the right to take over the home or household goods on death or at the end of the relationship (see Agell, 2003: 127).

So which model of reform would best suit the needs of cohabitants in England and Wales? In order better to protect cohabiting families, we take the view that the default position should protect the more vulnerable family members. After a specified period of time (two years would fit in with current statutory provisions relating to cohabitants), or on the birth of a child of the relationship, cohabitants would gain the same protection and privileges afforded married couples on relationship breakdown and on death. This would involve equalising the provisions of the Inheritance (Provision for Family and Dependants) Act 1975 by removal of the 'maintenance' stipulation (s1(2)(b)) and extending the remedies available to divorcing spouses in the MCA 1973 to cohabiting parents and cohabitants of, say, two years' standing. The discretion which is found in the criteria contained in s25 MCA 1973 and in s3 Inheritance Act 1975 would be sufficient to allow the courts to provide remedies appropriate to the particular cohabitation relationship in much the same way as they currently do with marriages. Short term cohabitants without children would get little or nothing. Longer term relationships or those with children of both parties would justify more distribution. This would also ensure that where children were concerned, their interests became the first consideration in the relationship breakdown context, that both financial and non-financial contributions to the welfare of the family were taken into account, and that issues of economic disadvantage and unjust enrichment could be redressed within the discretion.

This proposal would rid the law of much of its complexity and confusion by providing a cohesive family law-based framework for all families. In so doing vulnerable cohabitants and their children would gain better legal protection, and indirect discrimination against children of cohabiting relationships would be precluded. Furthermore, this proposal would remove perverse incentives not to marry. In addition, cohabitation should be recognised as a formal status and cohabitants should be regarded as each other's next of kin and be able to register the death of their partner. In this way family law would be better aligned with both people's expectations and their social practice. These outputs would not be achieved if a legal status providing similar but inferior family law regulation for cohabitants was introduced, as proposed by the Law Society (2002). Given that the law has already acknowledged cohabitants as suitable prospective adopters (Adoption and Children Act 2002), this approach would finalise the acceptance of longer term cohabitants as 'as good as married' and render the law much more cohesive and less illogical.

However, we should not ignore the need to safeguard the autonomy and preserve the freedom of choice of cohabitants who do not want to be treated as married. It should therefore be possible for a couple to opt out of this proposed regime, subject to some form of safety-net provision whereby children's interests are safeguarded and both partners can obtain independent legal advice. This ability to opt out could be achieved either by placing beyond doubt the lawfulness of cohabitation contracts as proposed in Scotland (Scottish Executive, 2000), or through combination with the operation of a French PaCS-style Civil Partnership Register which would provide cohabitants with a true alternative legal status to marriage. Those who are jointly deliberately seeking to avoid the implications of marriage are more likely, we suggest, to be economic equals and will be more motivated to take the appropriate steps than those who falsely believe they already have marriage-like rights. This exception would minimise oppression of those who wish to remain legally uncommitted as well as greatly reduce the perverse incentive for the wealthy not to marry.

The evidence presented in this book strongly indicates that the time has come for a functional approach to family regulation. This could, as has occurred in some Australian states, be framed so as to extend beyond cohabitation to other domestic relationships, should policy makers think fit (see Australian Capital Territory Domestic Relationships Act 1994 and the New South Wales Property (Relationships) Legislation Amendment Act 1999). Definitional problems can and have been overcome in other jurisdictions. For example, Australian legislation in both New South Wales and the Australian Capital Territory speaks of 'de facto marriage' which includes cohabitation relationships. This now also encompasses other 'domestic relationships' defined in the New South Wales context as any 'close personal relationship between two adult persons whether or nor related by family, who are living together one or each of whom provides the other with domestic support and personal care'. Section 3 of the New South Wales De Facto Relationships Act 1984 had originally been restricted to couples 'living together or having lived together as a husband and wife on a bona fide domestic basis although not married to each other.' Other definitions can be found in Canada where the term 'spouse' is extended to cohabitants (29 Ontario Family Law Act) and New Zealand where s2D Property Law (Amendment) Act 2001 defines cohabitants according to a list of criteria. This approach was also suggested by the Law Society in their 2002 consultation paper.

Both the BSA survey and the in-depth interviews showed strong support for equalisation of the rights of married couples and cohabitants, although views varied on the appropriate timeframe after which cohabitants should gain rights. Very few were in favour of a qualification period of more than three years, and the presence of children was seen by many as another appropriate independent trigger. As noted in chapter 1, during the 1970s and 1980s, English and Welsh law adopted elements of a functional approach in a predominantly form-based family law in order to prevent injustice to 'as good as married' cohabitants—albeit on an *ad hoc* basis. This was already a response to rather than a cause of *démariage*, but it has left the law complex, confused and out of line with social practice. To abandon a functional approach at this moment would leave social and legal norms dangerously apart. Rather we should accept that the protective aims of family law, as devised and developed cohesively for married couples, are now appropriate to the fast-growing numbers of functionally similar cohabiting families.

5 CONCLUSION

Our proposals for a plurality of responses might be construed as a call for what Gunther Teubner (1993) has termed 'reflexive law'. This, as Michael King and Christine Piper (1995: 36) explain:

> is offered as an answer to the crisis caused by the failure of legal rationality
> under modern conditions to provide law with the necessary tool to restore
> consensual, moral and political values.

Dewar (1998), drawing on Bourdieu's suggestion that the logic of following a rule ceases at the point at which logic ceases to be practical, looks to legal professionals to allay the chaos he identifies as inherent in family law in the case of divorce. He sees that broad discretionary principles allow the practitioner's pragmatism to be a guiding light. However, this is not a role that legal professionals— whose negotiation generally *is* undertaken in the shadow of the law (Mnookin and Kornhauser, 1979)—can easily perform for cohabitants. For here the law regulating disputes is often not governed by family law principles but rather by property law, tax law or social security law (as applied to unrelated strangers). This law tends to be starkly uncompromising and lacking discretion, as well as inconsistent. Unless we are prepared to concede that families are no longer in need of family law-style regulation (a view at odds with our research findings) and to reject the protective role that family law has played in regulating marriage, a cohesive legislative response to changing social norms in the family sphere is called for. Our findings lead us to conclude that a principled but not prescriptive legislative response is needed to regulate the 'normal chaos of love' (Beck and Beck-Gernsheim, 1995). To legislate in a pluralistic way would, we suggest, overcome the difficulties of regulating evolving and changing families in an area where otherwise the 'chaos of the law' will extend far beyond the normal.

To follow this conclusion also involves moving away from the dominant standard-setting role of legal norms (the form or status approach). Instead the law would take a neutral stance, which is prepared to be pragmatic, and admit that in the cohabitation context there is clear evidence that the prevailing social norm about justice requires that functionally alike families achieve equality before the law. In exchange, however, the law would lose much of the confusion and complexity resulting from the current indecision as to whether to favour a status- or function-based regulatory rationale. In addition, family law would gain a cohesion which is in line with good law-making principles. We do not argue that social attitudes and norms should guide the revision of legal norms in every law reform context, or that other public policy considerations should be abandoned. However, our research does point to the conclusion that this is the most appropriate response in this sphere—the law has little power to effectively impose a pro-marriage message in the absence of pro-marriage social norms. This response will undoubtedly require a fundamental shift away from the imposition of a top-down social morality, which is implied in the current government stance to these issues (see Blair, 1996 and Barlow and Duncan, 2000). Rather, it would effectively amount to giving common law marriage back to the people.

Appendix 1:
Research Design and Methods

1.1 THE EXTENSIVE RESEARCH—USING THE BRITISH SOCIAL ATTITUDES SURVEY

The British Social Attitudes Survey

The British Social Attitudes (BSA) survey is an annual national survey of attitudes, administered by the National Centre for Social Research, and designed to yield a representative sample of adults in Britain aged 18 and above. We had access to the 2000 survey, employing both specific questions for this research as well as using information from other 'standard' questions in the survey about social characteristics (like age, class, gender and occupation). Details of the 2000 BSA survey are available in Park et al, 2000. Because of differences in the legal situation in Scotland the research reported here used information from the 3,101 respondents living in England and Wales, but Anne Barlow has provided a detailed discussion about cohabitation in Scotland using the Scottish part of the survey (Barlow, 2002).

The fieldwork for the BSA survey was conducted using face-to-face computer assisted interviewing during June and September 2000, and achieved an overall response rate of 62 per cent. The data were weighted so as to reflect the selection probabilities at these three main stages, and all percentages referred to in this book are based on these weighted data. Information from the survey was collated and analysed using SPSS (Statistical Package for the Social Sciences). This is a computer programme with a wide range of facilities for data manipulation and analysis, ranging from simple descriptive features to more complex statistical tests and analysis techniques using factor analysis and regression analysis. Full details of this process are available in Park et al, 2000.

The BSA Cohabitation/Marriage Questions

For cohabitation and marriage, respondents were (1) asked face to face questions about their experiences and practices of, and attitudes about, cohabitation and marriage; (2) asked to return self-completion forms with further attitude questions relating to cohabitation; and (3) asked to respond, face to face, to scenario questions about cohabitation. These were as follows:

(1) Face to Face Questions:

ASK ALL LIVING AS MARRIED

Q761 Now a few questions about your household. Firstly, have you ever been married in the past?

ASK ALL MARRIED

Q762 Now a few questions about you and your household. Firstly, have you ever been married before now?

ASK ALL NOT CURRENTLY LIVING AS MARRIED

Q763 Now a few questions about you and your household. Have you and a (man/woman) ever lived together as a couple without being married?

ASK ALL CURRENTLY LIVING TOGETHER AS MARRIED OR EVER LIVED TOGETHER AS MARRIED IN THE PAST

Q764 IF CURRENTLY LIVING TOGETHER AS MARRIED:

About how long have you and your partner been living together as a couple?

IF LIVED TOGETHER AS MARRIED IN THE PAST

About how long did you live as a couple for with this (man/woman)? If you've lived as couple like this more than once, just tell us about the longest period.

Q765 IF CURRENTLY LIVING TOGETHER AS MARRIED: Do you or your partner own your accommodation?

IF YES: Do you own it jointly or not?

IF LIVED TOGETHER AS MARRIED IN THE PAST:

I now want to ask you a few questions about this time when you were living as a couple—again, think of the longest period if you've done this more than once. Firstly, did you or your partner ever own your accommodation while you were living together?

IF YES: Did you own it jointly or not?

IF 'owned jointly' or 'owned not jointly'

Q766 (Do/Did) you have (then) any written agreement with your partner other than a will or mortgage about your share in the ownership of your home?

ASK ALL CURRENTLY LIVING TOGETHER AS MARRIED OR EVER LIVED TOGETHER AS MARRIED IN THE PAST

Q767 (Have/Did) either you or your partner (made or changed/make or change) a will because you were living together as a couple?

Q768 IF CURRENTLY LIVING TOGETHER AS MARRIED: And, have you and your partner any children together?

IF LIVED TOGETHER AS MARRIED IN THE PAST: When you were living together as a couple with this (man/woman), did you and (he/she) have any children together? Again, please think of the partner you lived with for the longest period.

IF 'yes'

Q769 Some people who live together sign parental responsibility agreements or have parental responsibility orders decided by a court. Have you taken out these for any of your children by this partner?

ASK ALL WHO LIVED TOGETHER AS MARRIED IN THE PAST

Q770 Did you and this partner ever get married?

ASK ALL WHO HAVE NEVER LIVED TOGETHER AS MARRIED AND THOSE ANSWERING 'no'

Q771 Can I just check, have you ever (fathered a child/ given birth to a child)?

ASK ALL WITH CHILDREN

Q772 How old were you when your first child was born?

(2) Self-Completion Questions:

9. As far as you know, do unmarried couples who live together for some time have a 'common law marriage' which gives them the same legal rights as married couples?

10. Please tick one box to show how much you agree or disagree with each of these statements.

    a. People who want children ought to get married

    b. It is all right for a couple to live together without intending to get married

    c. It is a good idea for a couple who intend to get married to live together first

11. And please tick one box to show how much you agree or disagree with each of these statements.

    a. Married couples make better parents than unmarried ones

    b. Too many people just drift into marriage without really thinking about it

    c. Even though it might not work out for some people, marriage is still the best kind of relationship

    d. Many people who live together without getting married are just scared of commitment

    e. Marriage gives couples more financial security than living together

    f. There is no point getting married—it's only a piece of paper

(3) Scenario Questions:

Financial Support for Cohabitants   I'd now like you to imagine an unmarried couple with no children who have been living together for ten years. Say their relationship ends. Do you think the woman should or should not have the same rights to claim for financial support from the man as she would if they had been married?

And do you think she does in fact have …

… the same rights as a married woman to claim financial support from the man, or,

… does she have fewer rights?

Inheritance Rights   Imagine another unmarried couple without children who have been living together for ten years and live in a house bought in the man's name. Say he dies without making a will. Do you think the woman should or should not have the same rights to remain in this home as she would if she had been married to the man?

And do you think she does in fact have …

… the same rights as a married woman to remain in this home, or,

… does she have fewer rights?

Father's Rights   Now imagine another unmarried couple who have been living together for ten years. They have a child who needs medical treatment. Do you think the father should or should not have the same rights to make decisions about his child's medical treatment as he would if he was married to the child's mother?

And do you think he does in fact have …

… the same rights as a married man to make decisions about this medical treatment,

… or, does he have fewer rights?

1.2 THE INTENSIVE RESEARCH: THE FOLLOW-UP INTERVIEWS

Methods

The intensive research component of the study depends on 48 follow-up interviews with respondents who took part in the BSA survey conducted between

April and September 2001, supplemented by 25 interviews with British Asians and African-Caribbeans (see below for sampling). In all cases only one member of a couple was interviewed. Interviews were face-to-face and conducted at the interviewees' homes. The interviews were recorded (and later transcribed) and lasted between 60 and 90 minutes. We used semi-structured interviews, guided by a schedule, but using an open-ended conversational style of interviewing where interviewees could explain choices and reasoning as much as possible in their own language and within their own frameworks. 'Prompts' and 'pursues' were employed to introduce issues which we felt the respondent had not adequately covered. The schedule itself was developed through a pilot study of nine current and former cohabitants in the Aberystwyth area (two men and seven women) and in consultation with an Advisory Group of suitably qualified academics and legal practitioners. See Appendix 2 for a copy.

The interviews focused on three broad areas, as follows:

1 Practices of, experiences of, and attitudes to cohabitation/marriage.
2 Belief/lack of belief in common law marriage.
3 Views about legal reform.

For the 48 follow-up interviews we also had standard data from the original BSA survey.

Sampling: the BSA Follow-up Interviews

Our purposive sampling, using the BSA sample as a base, attempted to cover particular groups of cohabitant, or former cohabitant, where we expected that behaviour might differ in some way. These would often be overlapping so separate samples for each type of cohabitant were not necessary. These groups were:

Partnership Type and Parental Status
Current cohabitants with children, current cohabitants without children, cohabitants who had had children when cohabiting and gone on to marry that partner, former cohabitants who had had children together and were no longer together and now single, former cohabitants who had had children together and gone on to marry a new partner, those who were in their first partnership and those who were re-partnered.

Length of Cohabitation
Long term (two years or more) and short term (less than two years) cohabiting couples.

Legal Beliefs
Believers and non-believers in the common law marriage myth, those with and those without relevant legal provisions in place.

Social Divisions

Males and females, those with professional/managerial occupations, intermediate class and skilled working class occupations, and semi/unskilled occupations or long-term unemployed working class, renters and owner-occupiers (including those who rented/owned jointly and those where they were sole tenants/owners), people of Asian, Black and White ethnic groups.

There were difficulties in establishing interviews (some were unable/unwilling to take part because they worked long hours, were on holiday, were too busy, or in hospital, others were un-contactable, had moved or failed to turn up at the time of interview, or their circumstances had changed so that they were no longer suitable for the sample). Eventually, we conducted 48 interviews with BSA respondents. Their characteristics, in terms of categories outlined above, were as follows:

Partnership and Parental Status

- Twenty-seven current cohabitants with children.
- Eleven current cohabitants without children (of whom 4 had changed their relationship status by the time of the interview).
- Four former cohabitants with children who were lone parents.
- Five former cohabitants with children now married to their partner.
- One former cohabitant with children now married to a new partner.
- Twenty-nine cohabiting with their first partner and 19 re-partnered.

Length of Cohabitation

- Thirty-eight long term and 10 short term cohabitants.

Legal Beliefs

- Twenty-four 'believers' in common law marriage, 17 'non-believers', and five who were unsure (according to the BSA survey).
- Thirteen who had and 35 who did not have legal provisions in place.

Social Divisions

- Fifteen men and 33 women.
- Fifteen professionals, employers and managers, 22 intermediate/skilled workers, and 11 semi/unskilled/long-term unemployed working class.
- Twelve who were renting their homes (five jointly and seven as sole tenancies) and 36 owner occupiers (20 joint and 16 sole ownership).
- All were White.

The Ethnic Minority Group Interviews

As described in chapter 1, we took small additional interview samples, outside the BSA sample frame, of eight British African/African-Caribbean current and former cohabitants living in Lambeth and Southwark in Inner London, and 17 British Asians living in Bradford, in West Yorkshire. Interviewees were contacted using the snowballing technique, that is, following personal recommendations from an initial contact, during the summer/autumn of 2001. The interviews were conducted by interviewers from these specific ethnic groups and focused on issues raised in the original follow-up interview schedule (see Appendix 2). In addition, interviewees were also asked the attitudinal and scenario questions relating to cohabitation and marriage that were part of the original BSA survey (see above). For one Asian interviewee we only have information on the self-completion attitudinal questions.

The composition of the two ethnic groups varied. While the African/African-Caribbean group consisted, like the follow-up interviews, of current and former cohabitants this was not possible for the British Asians, given the extremely low levels of cohabitation amongst this group. The African/African-Caribbean group consisted of:

Partnership and Parental Status

    —Five current cohabitants (four with children).
    —Three former cohabitants (one of whom was married to her cohabiting partner and two of whom were single at the time of the interview.

Legal Beliefs

    —2 believers in common law marriage, 4 non-believers and 2 unsure.

Social Divisions

    —Three males and five females.
    —2 professionals, employers and managers, and 6 intermediate/skilled workers.
    —Four African and four African-Caribbean respondents.

The British Asian group consisted of:

Partnership and Parental Status

    —Five married, nine single (one of whom was a former cohabitant) and two divorcees.

Legal Beliefs

    —7 believers in common law marriage, 6 non-believers and 4 unsure.

Social Divisions

——Ten males and six females.
——6 professionals, 4 intermediate/skilled workers, and 4 semi/unskilled/
   long-term unemployed working class.
——Twelve Pakistani, three Indian and one Bangladeshi respondents.

Data Processing and Analysis

Interview recordings were transcribed into computer text by experienced tran-
scribers, and then some easily quantifiable information was processed and recorded using SPSS. However, the interviews were also entered onto, Nud*ist, a
software package designed for qualitative data analysis. This was used to establish and code differences and themes in the interviews (using 'nodes'). This cod-
ing was not predetermined although the broad themes of the interview schedule
were the same for all of the interviews. This in-depth information then provided
an information base for discussing cohabitants' practices, beliefs and understandings in depth, and also provided a source of illustrative statements from interviewees themselves.

Appendix 2: The Interview Schedule, Family Restructuring and Legal Realism

INTRODUCTION

My name is _____

I am looking at the ways families are changing in Britain, especially why more people are living together as a couple at some point in their life. I am interested in how people come to choose their family structures and what they know about how the law treats families outside marriage.

Thank you for agreeing to talk to me.

Everything you tell me will be completely anonymous. You won't be identified and we never pass on information about you or your family to anyone else.

The interview will take about an hour to an hour and a half of your time. I will be taping the interview but no one apart from the researchers will be able to listen to the tape.

GENERAL BACKGROUND AND COHABITATION/MARRIAGE QUESTIONS

1   Statistics show that there has been an increase in the number of people who live together as a couple without getting married. Does this tie in with your own experience/that of people you know or not?

If does—Why do you think this is the case? Why do you think we have seen such a general increase?
If not—Why not—why do you think your situation doesn't follow the trend?

2   Could you give me information about your current family situation/household?

Current Cohabitee—Q.3
Former Cohabitee—Married him/her?—Go to Q.28
Former Cohabitee—Separated from him/her and now married to new partner?—Go to Q.51
Former Cohabitee—Separated and now live alone (with the child or without the child?)—Go to Q.82

CURRENT COHABITEES

3   Can you tell me about your immediate family?

   How many of you live here in total? How old are you? And your partner? Do you and your partner have children together?
   Yes—How many children do you have together? Do you have any from a previous relationship? Does your partner? How old are they? Do they all live here?
   No—Do you have any children from a previous relationship? If yes—how many? How old are they—where do they live? Does your partner have any children from a previous relationship?
   Are you /your family religious?

4   (+Child Only) Did you and your partner register the birth(s) of your child(ren) jointly?

5   Have you changed your surname to that of your partner (or vice versa)?

   If yes, how was this done? By declaration (deed poll)? Why did you/your partner do it? When did you/your partner do it?

6   How long have you been living together as a couple?

   How long was it after you met that you decided to live together?

7   How long have you lived in this area?

   Were you/your partner from here originally? If not, where from?

8   Do you own the property or rent?

   Jointly or in your sole name—partner's sole name?
   (Owner Occupiers only)—do you have a written agreement about your shares in the home?

9   Do you work at the moment?

   Did you work? Does your partner? What jobs?—Part time or full time?
   Are you dependent on any welfare benefits? If yes, whom are they paid to?

10 How do you manage the household finances?

   Do you pool income? Who pays the mortgage/rent?

Do you have a joint bank account? Or does one pay bills, other pays rent/mortgage? Who's in control of the finances? Do you monitor your individual payments in and out of the account?

11 (+Child Only) Has having children affected your working life/career? or that of your partner?

How? How do you and your partner divide the childcare commitments/household chores?

12 Could you tell me about how you came to live together as a couple?

Eg Financial reasons/emotional reasons/stability/children/trial marriage?/ideological—reject marriage? How soon after you started the relationship was it that you decided to live together?

13 Have either of you ever cohabited or been married before?

If yes, how did this affect your decision to live together (positively or negatively)?

14 Have you ever considered getting married to each other?

Why/why not? What do you see as the pros and cons of getting married for your relationship?

If yes—What sort of wedding would you have? In church? Why is this important/not important? What about your partner—do you think he/she wants to get married? Is it something you have talked about? Do you think s/he wants a big wedding?

If no—do you want to get married at some point in your relationship/ever? Why/why not? If yes, what sort of wedding would you have? Does your partner want to get married?—have you discussed this?

15 How might/does having children influence the way you feel about marriage?

Why or why not?

16 (+Child) Whose surname does the child have (father's/mother's/joint)?

Why did you choose this? Do you think this is important—why/why not? Who decided that this was what you would do? Was it something you discussed? (If relevant) how do you think your children feel about this? Have you discussed it with them?

17 (–Child) If you have a child in the future whose surname would the child have?

Why? Do you think this is important? Is it something you have discussed with your partner? What do you think his/her views on this are? Would you register the birth of the child jointly? Have you thought about this? Do you think this is important? Is it something you have discussed with your partner? What do you think his/her views on this are?

18 (If religious) You said that you are religious earlier—how (if at all) has this influenced the way you/your partner feel about the fact that you're not married to your partner?

   Eg made you feel uneasy?

19 Is there anything that the Government could do that would persuade you to get married to each other?

   Eg Financial incentives (tax relief, wedding grant)?

20 What (other) factors might influence your decision to get married at some point in the future?

   Financial? Other people? Stability? Rebelling? Conforming?

21 Is living with someone and not being married accepted by your family?

   How do you think they feel about it? Have any other members of your family ever lived together as a couple? Do you think that the fact that you have/don't have children together affects the way your family feel about you being unmarried? What do they say?

22 What is their (your parents) background in terms of marriage?

   Always been married? How do you see their relationship? Do you think that's had any impact on your feelings towards marriage? What about your partner's parents?

23 How do you think your neighbours and others in the area that you have contact with feel about you not being married?

   Do they know or care do you think? Has anything ever been said to you? If yes, how did it make you feel?

24 Are most of your friends married or do they live together?

   Do they have children? How do you think they feel about the fact that you aren't married? Why? Does this affect your own views?

25 Do you ever find there are situations where you feel more comfortable being thought of as married?

   Eg (+Child) At the child's school—with teachers, other parents? At social gatherings (weddings?). If yes, how do you deal with this? Do you ever wear a ring on the third finger of your left hand to sug-gest that you are engaged/married? Does your partner? Why or why not?

26 (+Child) Do you think there have ever been times when your child has felt uncomfortable about you not being married?

   If yes, how did you deal with this?

27 Are you happy to continue living together?

   Indefinitely? Some people don't really feel secure in a relationship (eg its ability to last, faithfulness of your partner, are you confident that it will last) until they are married—is that something you can relate to?

Go to Q109

FORMER COHABITEES—MARRIED TO EACH OTHER NOW

28 Can you tell me about your immediate family?

How many of you live here in total? How old are you? And your partner? Do you and your partner have children together? How old are they? Do they all live here? Do you or your partner have any other children? Are you/your family religious?

29 When did you get married?

How long lived together prior to this?—Were the children born before you were married—did you and your partner register the birth(s) of your child(ren) jointly?

30 Did you change your surname to that of your partner when you married (or vice versa)?

Why/Why not?

31 How long have you lived in this area?

Were you/your partner from here originally? If not, where from?

32 Do you own the property or rent?

Jointly or in your sole name—partner's sole name? (Owner Occupiers only)—do you have a written agreement about your shares in the home?

33 Do you work at the moment?

Did you work? Full time or part time? What job? Does your husband/ wife? Are you dependent on any welfare benefits? If yes, who are they paid to? How changed over the years?

34 How do you manage the household finances?

Do you pool your incomes? Who pays the mortgage/rent? Do you have a joint bank account? How do you divide the household finances? (eg one pays bills, other pays rent/mortgage)? Who's in control of the finances? Do you monitor your individual payments in and out of the account?

35 Has having children affected your working life/career? or that of your partner?

In what way? How do you and your partner divide childcare commitments/household chores? Has this always been the case—changed since you got married? Why do you do things this way?

36 Could you tell me about how you initially came to live together as a couple?

Eg Financial reasons/emotional reasons/stability/children/trial mar-riage? Ideologically, reject marriage? How soon after you started the relationship was it that you decided to live together?

37 Had you or your partner ever cohabited or married before?

If yes, how did this affect your decision to live together (positively or neg-atively)?

38 Could you tell me about why you decided to get married?

Had it always been something that you wanted when you were living togeth-er as a couple? Is it something you talked about when you were living together? What were your views on the subject/your partner's views? Did they change over time (how, why?) Who proposed to whom? Was it a big wedding? Expensive? In a church or Register Office? How important was the wedding day itself to you? And your partner? Your children (if relevant)?

39 Did having or wanting children influence your decision to marry?

Why or why not?

40 Whose surname does the child have (father's/mother's/joint?)?

Why did you choose this? Do you think this is important—why? Who decid-ed that this was what you wanted to do? Was it something you discussed?

41 (If religious) For some people religious beliefs are very important influences in a decision to marry—has your religion had any influence on the decisions you've made?

How (if at all) has this influenced the way you/your partner feel about the fact that you're not married to your partner?
Eg made you feel uneasy?

42 When you were living together as a couple was it accepted by your family?

How do you think they felt about it? Do you think that your having children affects the way your family felt about you being married or unmarried? Have any other members of your family ever lived together as a couple? Do you think they are happier now that you are married? Why or why not?

43 What is their (your parents) background in terms of marriage?

Always been married? How do you see their relationship? Do you think that's had any impact on your feelings towards marriage? What about your partner's parents?

44 What about your neighbours and others in the area that you have contact with—how did they feel about you not being married?

Has anything ever been said to you? How did it make you feel? Do you feel more or less accepted now that you are married?

45 Are most of your friends married or do they live together?

Do they have children? How do you think they felt about the fact that you weren't married? Why? Have your group of friends changed since you got married? (eg more married couples with children?) How do their feelings affect your own views?

46 Before you were married, did you ever find that there were situations where you felt more comfortable being thought of as married?

What about at the child's school—with teachers, other parents? At social gatherings (eg weddings)? If yes, how did you deal with this? Did you ever wear a ring on the third finger of your left hand to suggest that you are engaged/married? Did your partner?

47 (If relevant) Do you think there was ever a time when your child felt uncomfortable about the fact that you were not married?

If yes, how did you deal with this?

48 How important would you say being married is to your relationship?

Why/why not? What do you see as the pros and cons of getting married for your relationship? How important is it to your partner? Your children? Are you more/less secure? More or less vulnerable in your relationship?

49 Do you think you are better off now or when you were living as a couple?

If yes, in what way? (emotionally, financially) Why? How do you think your partner feels about this? And your children (if relevant)?

50 Are you happier now that you're married?

Some people feel more secure in the relationship (eg its ability to last, faithfulness of your partner, are you confident that it will last) once they are married?

Go to Q109

FORMER COHABITEES—WHO MARRIED A NEW PARTNER

51 Can you tell me about your immediate family/household?

Who makes up your household?
How many children do you have?
How many are from a previous relationship? How old are they? Do they all live here? Does your husband/wife have any other children? Does your ex-partner?
How many in house?—who?—ages? How long were you living with your child's father/mother before you separated? How old are you? Your husband/wife? Are you religious?

52 Did you and your ex-partner register the birth(s) of your child(ren) jointly?

53 Have you changed your surname to that of your partner (or vice versa)?

> *If yes, how was this done? By declaration (deed poll)? Why did you/your partner do it? When did you/your partner do it?*

54 How long have you lived in this area?

> *Were you/your partner from here originally? If not, where from?*

55 Do you own the property or rent?

> *Jointly or in your sole name—partners sole name?*
> *(Owner Occupiers only)—do you have a written agreement about your shares in the home?*

56 Do you work at the moment?

> *Part time or full time? Does your husband/wife? Are you dependent on any welfare benefits? Who are they paid to?*

57 Do you receive/pay any maintenance from/to your ex-partner in relation to your child?

> *If not, was that something you discussed as parents? Why did you decide not to pay/receive maintenance?*

58 How do you manage the household finances?

> *Do you pool your income? Who pays the mortgage/rent? Do you have a joint bank account? How do you divide the household finances? (eg one pays bills, other pays rent/mortgage)? Who's in control of the finances? Do you monitor your individual payments in and out of the account?*

59 Has having children affected your working life/career? or that of your partner?

> *How? How do you and your partner divide the childcare responsibilities/household chores? Why that way?*

60 How were you supported financially in the previous relationship (when you were living together as a couple with the father/mother of your child)?

> *Did you work? Did your partner? Were you dependant on any benefits then? Who were they paid to?*

61 Was the property you lived in then owned or rented?

> *Jointly or in your sole name—ex-partner's sole name?*
> *(Owner Occupiers only)—did you have a written agreement about your shares in the home?*

62 And how did you manage the household finances in that relationship?

> *Did you pool your income then? Who paid the mortgage/rent? Did you have a joint bank account? How did you divide the household finances? (eg one*

paid bills, other paid rent/mortgage)? Who was in control of the finances? Did you monitor your individual payments in and out of the account?

63 Did having children affect your or your ex-partner's ability to work at that time?

How? How did you divide the childcare responsibilities/household chores then?

64 Could you tell me about how you came to live with your ex-partner as a couple?

Eg Financial reasons/emotional reasons/stability/children/trial marriage/ideological reasons—reject marriage? How soon after you started the relationship was it that you decided to live together?

65 Had you or your ex-partner ever been married or cohabited in the past?

If yes, how did this affect your decision to live together (positively or negatively)?

66 Did you ever consider marrying him/her?

Why/why not? Did your ex-partner ever want to get married? (was it something you discussed?) Did your child want you to get married (if relevant)? What did you see as the pros and cons of getting married for that relationship?

67 Do you think it would have made a difference to that relationship if you had been married?

Why/why not? If yes, in what way (negative/positive effect)?

68 Did having a child together affect the way you felt about getting married?

Why or why not? Whose surname does the child have (father's/mother's/joint)? Why did you choose this? Did you discuss this? Whose decision was that?

69 (If religious) For some people religious beliefs are very important influences in a decision to marry—has your religion had any influence on the decisions you've made?

How (if at all) has this influenced the way you/your partner feel about the fact that you're not married to your partner?
Eg made you feel uneasy?

70 Is there anything the Government could have done that would have persuaded you to marry each other?

Eg Financial incentives (tax relief/wedding grant)?

71 When you were living together as a couple was it accepted by your family?

How do you think they felt about it? Have any other members of your family ever lived with someone as a couple? Do you think that your having a child together affected the way your family felt about you being unmarried?

72 What is their (your parents) background in terms of marriage?

Always been married? How do you see their relationship? Do you think that's had any impact on your feelings towards marriage? What about your partner's parents?

73 What about your neighbours and others in the area that you had contact with then?

Has anything ever been said to you? How did it make you feel? Do you feel more or less accepted now that you are married?

74 Were most of your friends at this time married or did they live together?

Did they have children? How do you think they felt about the fact that you weren't married? Why?

75 During that time, did you ever find that there were situations where you felt more comfortable being thought of as married?

What about at the child's school—with teachers, other parents? At social gatherings (weddings?). If yes, how did you deal with this? Did you ever wear a ring on the third finger of your left hand to suggest that you are engaged/married? Did your partner?

76 Do you think there were any times when your child felt uncomfortable?

If yes, how did you deal with this?

77 What happened when that relationship broke down?

Did you seek legal advice? If yes, from whom? When? Why? What was said? If not, why not? How were things resolved?

78 Since then, you have met and married a new partner. Did you live with your husband/wife before you married each other?

Why/why not? If yes, for how long? Whose decision was it to live together?

79 Could you tell me why you decided to marry him/her?

How important was it in this relationship? What do you see as the pros and cons of getting married for your relationship? To whom was it important? Did you discuss it? How do you think your children felt about it? When in the relationship did it become important? Who proposed to whom? Did you have a big wedding? How important was the type of wedding ceremony?

80 Are most of your friends married now or do they live together?

Do they have children? Does this affect your own views?

81 Are you happier being married?

Do you feel more/less secure? More or less vulnerable? Why? How do you think your husband/wife feels about this? And your children?

Go to Q109

FORMER COHABITEE—NOT MARRIED AND NO NEW PARTNER

82 Can you tell me about your immediate family/household?

Who makes up your household?
How many in the house?—ages? How long were you living together before you separated? And you have been alone for how long? How old are you? How many children do you have?
How old are they? Do they all live here? Does your ex-partner have any other children?
Are you religious?

83 Did you register the birth(s) of the child(ren) jointly?

84 Have you changed your surname to that of your partner (or vice versa)?

If yes, how was this done? By declaration (deed poll)? Why did you/your partner do it? When did you/your partner do it?

85 How long have you lived in this area?

Were you/your ex-partner from here originally? If not, where from?

86 Do you own the property or rent?

Jointly or in your sole name?
(Owner Occupiers only)—do you have a written agreement about your shares in the home?

87 What contact arrangements are in place for the child(ren)?

Without the child—how often do you see the child?
With child—does the child see his/her father/mother?

88 Do you work at the moment?

Part-time or full time? Are you dependent on any welfare benefits?

89 Do you pay/are you paid maintenance to/from the child's mother/father?

If not, why not?

90 Has having children affected your working life/career?

How?

91 How was the family supported financially when you were living with the child's father/mother?

Did you work? Did your partner? Were you dependent on any welfare benefits? Who were they paid to?

92 Did you own the property you lived in then or rent it?

> *Jointly or in your sole name—partner's sole name?*
> *(Owner Occupiers only)—did you have a written agreement about your*
> *shares in the home?*

93 How did you manage the household finances?

> *Did you pool your income? Who paid the mortgage/rent? Did you have a*
> *joint bank account? How did you divide the household finances? (eg one*
> *paid bills, other paid rent/mortgage)? Who was in control of the*
> *finances? Did you monitor your individual payments in and out of the*
> *account?*

94 Did having a child affect your ability or your partner's ability to work then?

> *How? How did you divide the childcare responsibilities/household*
> *chores? Why that way?*

95 Could you tell me about how you and your ex-partner came to live together
    as a couple?

> *Eg Financial reasons/emotional reasons/stability/children/trial mar-*
> *riage/ideological reasons—reject marriage? How soon after you started*
> *the relationship was it that decided to live together?*

96 Had you or your partner ever cohabited or been married before?

> *If yes, how did this affect your decision to live together (positively or neg-*
> *atively)?*

97 During the time that you were living together as a couple, did you ever con-
    sider getting married?

> *Why or why not? What did you see as the pros and cons of getting mar-*
> *ried for that relationship? If yes, did you want a white wedding? In*
> *Church? Why/why not? How important would the wedding day have been*
> *to you?*
> *What about your partner—do you think he/she wants to get married? Is*
> *it something you talked about? Do you think your child (if relevant) want-*
> *ed you to get married to each other?*

98 Do you think it would have made a difference to that relationship if you had
    been married?

> *Why/why not? If yes, in what way (negative/positive affect)?*

99 Did having a child influence the way you felt about marriage?

> *Why or why not? Whose surname does the child have (father's/moth-*
> *er's/joint?)? Why did you choose this? How important is this?*
> *Why/why not? Whose decision was this and how was it reached?*

100 (If religious) For some people religious beliefs are very important influences in a decision to marry—has your religion had any influence on the decisions you've made?

> *How (if at all) has this influenced the way you/your partner feel about the fact that you're not married to your partner?*
> *Eg made you feel uneasy?*

101 Is there anything that the Government could have done that would have persuaded you to marry each other?

> *Financial incentive (tax relief or wedding grant)?*

102 When you were living together as a couple was it accepted by your family?

> *How do you think they felt about it? Have any other members of your family ever lived with someone as a couple? Do you think that your having a child together affected the way your family felt about you being unmarried?*

103 What is their (your parents) background in terms of marriage?

> *Always been married? How do you see their relationship? Do you think that's had any impact on your feelings towards marriage? What about your partner's parents?*

104 What about your neighbours, friends and others in the area that you have contact with—how do you think they felt about the fact that you were living together?

> *Was anything ever said to you? How did it make you feel?*

105 When you were with your former partner, did you ever find that there were situations where you felt more comfortable being thought of as married?

> *What about at the child's school—with teachers, other parents? At social gatherings (weddings?). If yes, how did you deal with this? Did you ever wear a ring on the third finger of your left hand to suggest that you are engaged/married? Did your partner?*

106 Do you think there were ever times when your child felt uncomfortable?

> *If yes, how did you deal with it? What about now?*

107 What happened when that relationship broke down?

> *Did you seek legal advice? If yes, from whom? When? Why? What was said?*
> *If not, why not? How were things resolved?*

108 If you met somebody new—do you think you would get married or not?

> *Why or why not? Feel more secure/less secure? More or less vulnerable?*

Would you live with someone again? Why/why not? If yes, is there any-thing you would do differently?

Go to Q109

GENERAL QUESTIONS

I would now like to hear your views about different families living in Britain today and your understanding of the legal position of married and unmarried couples.

109 What do you think society in general feels about unmarried couples who live together?

More tolerant or less tolerant nowadays? Why/Why not?

110 What about unmarried couples with children? How do you think people in general feel about them?

Are they thought of any differently to married couples with children? Should they be? Why/why not?

111 You've been good enough to tell us about the particular choices that you have made—Why do you think people in general might choose to live together rather than marry each other?

Fear of commitment? Fear of losing independence? Try out the relation-ship? Financial? Ideological reasons (rejection of marriage)? Do you think these are good reasons—why/why not? What do you think are the advan-tages of marriage? What are the disadvantages? Can you think of any?

112 Why do you think people might choose to marry rather than live together as a couple?

More stability? Children? Parental pressure? Romanticism? Financial reasons? Symbolism? Wanting a sense of belonging? Surer about the relationship? What are the advantages/disadvantages?

113 How important do you think the wedding itself is to people who do want to marry?

Do you think the big white wedding is still important? Do you think people distinguish between the wedding ceremony and marriage? Why/why not?

114 Do you think that relationships between unmarried couples who live togeth-er are considered to be as serious as that of married couples?

Why/why not? Do you think we should consider them to be as serious as a married relationship—why/why not?

110 Check from BSA information whether believes in common law marriage or not? Or ask if no self-completion questionnaire.

Common Law Marriage Believers—Go to Q 111
Not Common Law Marriage Believers—Go to Q 114

BELIEVES IN COMMON LAW MARRIAGE

111 (Ask all where not married to former partner). In the original BSA survey you suggested that you definitely/probably believe in common law marriage (ie that unmarried couples who live together have the same legal rights and responsibilities as married couples). Does/did this idea of common law marriage affect your decision not to marry your partner/ex-partner?

Ie because you have the same rights and responsibilities as married couples anyway? Do you think this was in your mind at all? Why/why not? Do/did you ever think about it/discuss it with your partner/ex-partner?

112 Can you remember where and when you first heard about this idea of a 'common law marriage'?

Did someone tell you (if so who?)—is it something you 'just know'? Is it something that you have discussed as a couple/did you ever discuss this with your ex-partner? Or with friends or family? In relation to other people's relationships or your own? If yes, when did you discuss it (before you moved in together, once living together, after a time, on having a child)? What were his/her views?

113 So, as far as you're aware unmarried couples who live together have the same legal rights as married couples ... Look at scenario cards and answers given regarding whether should and do have same legal rights—ask if answer same if different time scales.

    a Scenario 1: Financial support for an unmarried partner?—Should and could?

    b Scenario 2: Rights re home on death of a partner?—Should and could?

    d Scenario 3: Father and child's medical treatment?—Should and could?

At what point in the relationship of the unmarried couple do you think these 'equal' rights take effect—eg as soon as they live together? After a year? Two years?

At what point do you think they should take effect?

114 Have you/did you ever feel you ought to check your legal position as a cohabitee—have you ever sought legal advice (eg from a CAB or solicitor) in relation to any of these issues?

If yes, when and what prompted you to do so? (eg when you bought the family home/when you moved in together/when child was born/when separated?)

Who did you see? (eg own solicitor/CAB) What advise did they give you? Did you follow it? Why/Why not?

If not, why not? Not important? Impact on relationship (suggests doubting it)?

Have you ever spoken to your partner/ex-partner about any of these issues?

If yes, when in your relationship did you discuss this? What were/are your partner's/ex-partner's views? Ever spoken to friends or family?

Go to Q123

DOES NOT BELIEVE IN COMMON LAW MARRIAGE

115 Do you know whether people who live together and have children together have equal rights and responsibilities in relation to the child in the same way as married parents?

> *Don't know—What would you imagine people's rights would be in this situation?*
>
> *(Eg consent to medical treatment/duty to maintain them financially/choose their school/register the birth/consent to school trips?)*
>
> *If yes, have same rights—What makes you think that?—Where or how did you learn that information? (eg common knowledge? Told (by whom?)? Read it?) (+Child) Have you and your partner/ex-partner ever discussed this? If yes, what were his/her views?*
>
> *If no, do not have same rights—What is your understanding of the situation then? Where or how did you learn that information? (eg common knowledge? Told (by whom?)? Read it?*
>
> *(+Child) Have you and your partner/ex-partner ever discussed this? If yes, what were his/her views?*

116 As far as you know does the joint registration of a child's birth have any legal effect on a parents rights and responsibilities towards the child?

> *Don't know—what do you think the situation might be?*
>
> *Yes/no—What's your understanding of the situation? How do you know this? Where from?*
>
> *(+Child) Why did you or why didn't you register the birth of your child jointly? Who decided that this was what you would do? Was it something you discussed? (if relevant) how do you think your children feel about this? Have you discussed it with them?*

117 Have you ever heard of parental responsibility agreements or orders?

> *If no—go to next question*
>
> *If yes—what is your understanding of them and how they work? Where or how did you hear about them?*
>
> *(+Child) Do you have one in relation to your child/children? If yes, why and how did this come about? If no, why not? Have you ever sought legal*

advice on this? If yes, when and what prompted you to do so? Did you and your partner discuss it? Whose idea was it to get one/not to get one? What were your partner's views?

118 Do you think that law relating to tax and welfare benefits favours married (as opposed to unmarried) couples with children or not?

Don't know—What do you imagine the case to be?
If no—what is your understanding? All treated the same? Where or how did you learn this?
If yes—what do you know? Where or how did you learn about this? Have you and your partner/ex-partner discussed it? What are or were his/her views?
Have you ever received professional advice about these issues? If yes, from whom, when, where and why?

119 Do you know whether unmarried couples get the same state pension rights as married couples?

Don't know—What do you imagine the case to be?
What about private schemes? Have you looked at this at any point? If yes, when? What do you know about it? What made you look into it?
Have you ever received professional advise about pensions? If yes, from whom, when, where and why?

120 As far as you know when a relationship breaks down, do unmarried couples have the same legal rights and responsibilities as married couples?

Eg In relation to their family home and maintenance of their partner?
Don't know—What would you imagine the situation to be?
Yes/no—How or where did you learn this information? Do you think the situation is any different if the couple have children? At what point in the relationship of an unmarried couple do you think these rights exist? (as soon as live together? After a year? Two years? Once have children?)
Is this something you have discussed with your partner/discussed with your ex-partner? If yes, when did you discuss this? What provisions have you or did you have in place to deal with this? (Eg ownership agreement in relation to the property?) Have you ever taken or thought about taking legal advice in relation to your own situation? If yes, when, in relation to what and why? What happened?

121 In terms of inheritance, do you know what would happen to the property of a cohabitee were s/he to die?

Automatically goes to his or her partner? Goes to any children? How do you know this? Where did hear about this?
What happens to the family home? Do you know? Is there any difference when the person who dies owns the family home to where s/he rents it?

Do you think cohabitees need to make a will any more than a married couple do?

Do you have any provisions in place to deal with this (eg changed your will)? Has your partner? If yes, when did you do this—what prompted you? Have you ever sought legal advice about this? If yes, when and why? What prompted you to do this? If not, why not?

Have you ever discussed this with your partner/or did you ever discuss this with your ex-partner? If yes, what are his/her views on this?

122 Have you ever discussed any of these issues with friends or family?

In relation to your situation or somebody elses?
If yes, when? What was said? If not, why not?

LAW REFORM

123 Do you think that all married and unmarried couples should have the same legal rights and responsibilities?

Why/why not? Does your answer apply to all legal rights (eg to property upon the death of one partner? In relation to children? Pensions? Benefits?)

124 What do you think about the idea that couples should have to live together for a certain amount of time before they have the same rights and responsibilities as married couples?

If think good idea, how long should that length of time be? Why at this point?
If don't—why not?
What about if they have children? Would your answer be different then? Why/why not? Should there be a time qualification at this point or should it just arise at the time of the birth?

125 There are examples of how the law deals with this issue in other countries— I would be interested to hear your views about these. For example there is the idea that couples who live together can sign a legal agreement which is filed at the local court and sets out certain rights and responsibilities that they agree to (eg in relation to how they own property). This can be terminated by notice and, if they sign the agreement they get the similar social security, inheritance and tax advantages as married couples. It means that those who sign it (and only those who sign it) are treated more or less as married in the eyes of the law. What do you think about that idea?

Do you think it would work here in the UK? Why/why not?
Current Cohabitants—Would you be willing to sign such an agreement? Do you think your partner would? Why/why not? If yes, what particular issues

would you like to have included in such a legally enforceable document? What do you see as the pros? And do you see any negative aspects?

Former Cohabitants—Would this have been something that you would have liked to have had in place when you were living with your ex-partner? Why/ why not?

If yes, what particular issues would you like to have included in such a legally enforceable document? What do you see as the pros? And do you see any negative aspects?

126 Another alternative is to formalise common law marriage through legislation – so parliament could issue a law saying that all those who live together after one year are treated as married. What do you think about that?

Would you set it at one year? Do you think you should be allowed to opt out of such a system? What about if the couple have children?

127 A more radical alternative is to abolish marriage. What do you think about that idea?

Have we reached a time where we can we abolish it?
Do we still want it? Is it important? Why/why not? If yes, to whom is it important? Will it always be important do you think?

128 There has been a lot of talk recently about how marriage is the best family structure within which to have and raise children. What do you think about this?

Is it something you have discussed with your partner ex-partner? What is important? What do you think makes a 'good' environment to bring up children?

129 Do you think that it would make people get married if the Government introduced financial incentives to do so?

Why or why not? What sort of incentives might influence people? (tax relief, wedding grant?)

130 What (other) things do you think the Government could do to convince people to get married?

Why? Eg better maternity or paternity leave for married couples only? Tax relief or paid childcare for married couples only, where one looks after the child?

131 Do you think that the Government should try and persuade couples to get married?

Why/why not? Do you see marriage as a private issue or as something that all of society has a say in? What about, where children are involved?

132 Finally, is there anything I haven't asked you about living with someone as a couple, your decision to get/not to get married or the relevant legal situation that you think is important and would like to add?

References

Agell, A (2003) 'The Legal Status of Same-Sex Couples in Europe – A Critical Analysis' in K Boele-Woelki and A Fuchs (eds), *Legal Recognition of Same-Sex Couples in Europe* (Antwerp: Intersentia)

Bailey, M (2004) 'Regulation of Cohabitation and Marriage in Canada' 26(1) *Law and Policy* 153–175

Bailey-Harris, R (1996) 'Law and the Unmarried Couple – Oppression or Liberation?' 8(2) *Child and Family Law Quarterly* 137–147

—— (2001) 'Dividing the Assets on Family Breakdown: The Content of Fairness' in Freeman, M (ed), *Current Legal Problems* (Oxford, Oxford University Press)

Barlow, A (1998) 'Family Structuring, Legal Regulation and Gendered Moral Rationalities: Some Empirical Findings', paper presented to Socio-Legal Studies Association Annual Conference, Manchester Metropolitan University, 16 April

Barlow, A (2001) *Cohabitants and the Law* (London, Butterworths)

—— (2002) 'Cohabitation and Marriage in Scotland: Attitudes, Myths and the Law' in J Curtice, D McCrone, A Park and L Paterson (eds), *New Scotland; New Society?* (Edinburgh: Edinburgh University Press)

—— (2004) 'Regulation of Cohabitation, Changing Family Policies and Social Attitudes: A Discussion of Britain within Europe' 26(1) *Law and Policy* 57–86

Barlow, A and Duncan, S (2000) 'Family Law, Moral Rationalities and New Labour's Communitarianism: Part II' 22(2) *Journal of Social Welfare and Family Law* 129–143

Barlow, A and James, G (2004) 'Regulating Marriage and Cohabitation in 21st Century Britain' 67(2) *Modern Law Review* 143–176

Barlow, A, Duncan, S, James, G and Park, A (2001) 'Just a Piece of Paper? Marriage and Cohabitation in Britain' in A Park, J Curtice, K Thomson, L Jarvi and C Bromley (eds), *British Social Attitudes: The 18th Report* (London: Sage)

Bauman, Z (1991) *Modernity and Ambivalence* (Cambridge, Polity Press)

Beck, U (2002) 'Zombie Categories; Interview with Ulrich Beck' in U Beck and E Beck-Gernsheim, *Individualisation* (London, Sage)

Beck, U and Beck-Gernsheim, E (1995) *The Normal Chaos of Love* (Cambridge, Polity Press)

Beck-Gernsheim, E (2002) *Reinventing the Family: In Search of New Lifestyles* (Cambridge, Polity)

Bissett-Johnson, A and Barton, C (1999) 'The Similarities and Differences in Scottish and English Family Law in Dealing with Changing Family Patterns' 21(1) *Journal of Social Welfare and Family Law* 1–21

Björnberg, U (2001) 'Cohabitation and Marriage in Sweden – Does Family Form Matter?' 15 *International Journal of Law, Policy and the Family* 350–362

Blair, A (1996) Foreword, in G Radice (ed), *What Needs to Change? New Visions for Britain* (London: HarperCollins)

Boele-Woelki, K (2003) 'Registered Partnerships and Same-Sex Marriage in the Netherlands' in K Boele-Woelki and A Fuchs, *Legal Recognition of Same-Sex Couples in Europe* (Antwerp, Intersentia)

Bowman, C (2004) 'Legal Treatment of Cohabitation in the United States' 26(1) *Law and Policy* 119–151

Brown, S and Booth, A (1996) 'Cohabitation versus Marriage: a comparison of relationship quality' 58 *Journal of Marriage and the Family* 668–678

Carbone, J (1996) 'Feminism, Gender and the Consequences of Divorce' in M Freeman (ed), *Divorce: Where Next?* (Aldershot, Dartmouth)

Carbone, J and Brinig, M (1991) 'Rethinking Marriage: Feminist Ideology, Economic Change and Divorce Reform' 65 *Tulane Law Review* 953–1006

Carling, A (2002) 'Family Policy, Social Theory and the State' in A Carling, S Duncan and R Edwards (eds), *Analysing Families: Morality and Rationality in Policy and Practice* (London: Routledge)

Casals, M (2003) 'Same-Sex Partnerships in the Legislation of the Spanish Autonomous Communities' in K Boele-Woelki and A Fuchs (eds), *Legal Recognition of Same-Sex Couples in Europe* (Antwerp, Intersentia)

Cleaver, F (2002) 'Reinventing Institutions: Bricolage and the Social Embeddedness of Natural Resource Management' 14(2) *European Journal of Development Research* 11–30

Coombs, L and Zumeta, Z (1970) 'Correlates of Marital Dissolution in a Prospective Fertility Study: A Research Note' 18 *Social Problems* 92–101

Cretney, S (2000) *Family Law: Essays for the New Millennium* (Bristol, Jordans)

Davies, C (1999) 'The Definition of Cohabitation' 79 *Solicitors Family Law Association Review* 15–16

Deech, R (1980) 'The Case Against Legal Recognition of Cohabitation' 29 *International Comparative Law Quarterly* 480

—— (1990), 'Divorce Law and Empirical Studies' 106 *Law Quarterly Review* 229

Dennis, N and Erdos, G (1992) *Families without Fatherhood* (London, Institute for Economic Affairs)

Department of Trade and Industry Women and Equality Unit (2003a) *Civil Partnership: A Framework for the Legal Recognition of Same-Sex Couples* (London, Department of Trade and Industry)

—— (2003b) *Responses to Civil Partnership: A Framework for the Legal Recognition of Same-Sex Couples* (London, Department of Trade and Industry)

Dewar, J (1998) 'The Normal Chaos of Family Law' 61 *Modern Law Review* 467–485

Dyer, M (2002) 'Property Rights Warning for Unmarried Couples' *The Guardian*, 19 July

Eekelaar, J (1984) *Family Law and Social Policy* (London, Weidenfeld and Nicholson)

—— (2000) 'Family Law and the Responsible Citizen' in M Maclean (ed), *Making Law for Families* (Oxford, Hart)

—— (2001) 'Asset Distribution on Divorce: the Durational Element' 117 *Law Quarterly Review* 552–560

Eekelaar, J and Maclean, M (1990) 'Divorce Law and Empirical Studies. A Reply' 106 *Law Quarterly Review* 621–631

—— (2004) 'Marriage and the Moral Bases of Personal Relationships' 31(4) *Journal of Law and Society* 510–539

Ermisch, J (2002) 'Trying Again: repartnering after dissolution of a union' *Working Paper of the Institute for Social and Economic Research*, paper 19 (Colchester, University of Essex)

Ermisch, J and Francesconi, M (1999) 'Cohabitation in Great Britain: not for long but here to stay' *Working Paper of the Institute for Social and Economic Research* (Colchester, University of Essex)

Evans, M (2003) *Love: An Unromantic Discussion* (Cambridge, Polity)

Ewick, P and Silbey, S (1992) 'Conformity, Contestation and Resistance: an account of legal consciousness' 26 *New England Law Review* 731–747

Finch, J (2004) 'Family Policy and Civil Registration in England and Wales' 33(2) *Journal of Social Policy* 249–266

Fineman, M (1991) *The Illusion of Equality: The Rhetoric and Reality of Divorce Reform* (Chicago, University of Chicago Press)

Fox Harding, L (1996) *Family, State and Social Policy* (Basingstoke, Macmillan)

Freeman, M (1984) 'Legal Ideologies, Patriarchal Precedents, and Domestic Violence' in M Freeman (ed), *The State, the Law and the Family: Critical Perspectives* (London, Tavistock)

Fukuyama, F (1999) *The Great Disruption* (New York, Free Press)

Galanter, M (1992) 'Law Abounding: Legislation around the North Atlantic' 55 *Modern Law Review* 55 1–24

Gibson, C (2000) 'Changing Family Patterns in England' in N Katz, J Eekalaar and M Maclean (eds), *Cross Currents: Family Law and Policy in the US and England* (Oxford, Oxford University Press)

Giddens, A (1992) *The Transformation of Intimacy: Sexuality, Love and Eroticism in Modern Societies* (Cambridge, Polity Press)

—— (1999) *Runaway World: How Globalisation is Shaping Our Lives* (London, Profile)

Gillis, J (1985) *For Better, For Worse. British Marriages 1600 to the Present* (Oxford, Oxford University Press)

—— (1997) *A World of their Own Making: a History of Myth and Ritual in Family Life* (Oxford, Oxford University Press)

Glendon, M (1981) *The New Family and the New Property* (Toronto: Butterworths)

Gonzalez-Lopez, M-J and Solsona, M (2000) 'Households and Families: changing living arrangements and gender relations' in S Duncan and B Pfau-Effinger (eds), *Gender, Work and Culture in the EU* (London, Routledge)

Hale, B (2004) 'Unmarried Couples in Family Law' 6 *Family Law* 419–426

Haskey, J (1983) 'Marital Status and Age at Marriage: their influence on the chance of divorce' 32 *Population Trends* 4–14

—— (1999) 'New Estimates and Projections of the Population Cohabiting in England and Wales' 95 *Population Trends* 1–17

—— (2001) 'Cohabitation in Great Britain: past, present and future trends – and attitudes' 103 *Population Trends* 4–25

Hibbs, M, Barton, C and Beswick, J (2001) 'Why Marry? Perceptions of the Affianced' *Family Law* 197–207

Hodgson, D (2000) 'My Daughter Belongs to the Government Now' in C Creighton and CK Omori (eds), *Gender, Family and Work in Tanzania* (London, Ashgate)

Home Office (1998) *Supporting Families: A Consultative Document* (London, The Stationery Office)

—— (2002) *Civil Registration: Vital Change* (London, The Stationery Office)

Johnson, D (2003) 'Publish or be Damned' *History Today,* November, 39–45

Johnson, M (1991) 'Commitment to Personal Relationships' in W Jones and D Penman (eds), *Advances in Personal Relationships: A Research Annual,* vol 3 (London, Jessica Kingsley)

Kiernan, K 'Unmarried Cohabitation and Parenthood in Britain and Europe' 26(1) *Law and Policy* 33–55

Kiernan, K and Estaugh, V (1993) *Cohabitation, Extra-marital Childbearing and Social Polic,* (York, Joseph Rowntree Foundation)

King, M and Piper, C (1995) *How the Law Thinks about Children* (Aldershot, Arena)

Laslett, P, Osterveen, K and Smith, R (eds) (1980) *Bastardy and its Comparative History* (London, Arnold)

Laurie, H and Gershuny, J (2000) 'Couples, Work and Money' in R Berthoud and J Gershuny (eds), *Seven Years in the Lives of British Households* (Bristol, Policy Press)

Law Commission (2002) *Sharing Homes: A Discussion Paper* (London, Law Commission for England and Wales)

Law Society (2002) *Cohabitation: the Case for Clear Law* (London, Law Commission for England and Wales)

Lesthaeghe, R (1995) 'The Second Demographic Transition in Western Countries: an Interpretation' in K Mason and A-M Jensen (eds), *Gender and Family Change in Industrialised Countries* (Oxford, Clarendon Press)

Lewis, C, Papacosta, A and Warin, J (2002) *Cohabitation, Separation and Fatherhood* (York, Joseph Rowntree Foundation)

Lewis, J (1999) *Marriage, Cohabitation and the Law: Individualism and Obligation* (London, Lord Chancellor's Department Research Series, No 1)

—— (2001) *The End of Marriage? Individualism and Intimate Relationships* (Cheltenham, Edward Elgar)

Maclean, M and Eekelaar, J (1997) *The Parental Obligation* (Oxford, Hart)

Medus, S (1989) *Toleration and the Limits of Liberalism* (London, Macmillan Press)

Mnookin, R and Kornhauser, L (1979) 'Bargaining in the Shadow of the Law: the Case of Divorce' 88 *Yale Law Journal* 950

Morgan, P (1999) *Marriage-lite: the Rise of Cohabitation and its Consequences* (London, Institute for the Study of Civil Society)

Murphy, M (1985) 'Demographic and Socio-economic Effects on Recent British Marital Breakdown Patterns' 39 *Population Studies*

Murray, C (1994), *Underclass: The Crisis Deepens*, Health and Welfare Unit, Choice in Welfare Series No 20 (London, Institute of Economic Affairs)

National Statistics (2004) *Living in Britain. The 2002 General Household Survey,* National Statistics Online, www.statistics.gov.uk

Nock, SL (1995) 'Commitment and Dependency in Marriage' 57 *Journal of Marriage and the Family* 503–514

O'Donovan, K (1993) *Family Law Matters* (London, Pluto Press)

Odgard, R (2002) 'Scrambling for Land in Tanzania' 14(2) *European Journal of Development Research* 70–88

Office for National Statistics (2000) *Social Trends 30* (London, The Stationery Office)

—— (2003) *Social Trends 33* (London, The Stationery Office)

Park, A (2000) 'The Generation Game' in R Jowell, J Curtice, A Park, K Thomson, J Jarvis, C Bromley and N Stratford (eds) *British Social Attitudes: the 17th Report – Focusing on Diversity* (London, Sage)

Park, A, Curtice, J, Thomson, K, Jarvis, L and Bromley, C (2000) (eds) *British Social Attitudes: The 18th Report* (London, Sage)

Parker, S (1998) *New Balances in Family Law* (Melbourne, Griffith University)

Phillips, M (2001) 'Home Truths they Conceal about Unmarried Couples' *The Sunday Times,* 2 December

Pickford, R (1999) *Fathers, Marriage and the Law* (London: Family Policy Studies Centre)

Prinz, C (1995) *Cohabiting, Married or Single* (Aldershot, Avebury)

Probert, R (2001) 'From Lack of Status to Contract: assessing the French *Pacte Civil de Solidarité*' 23(3) *Journal of Social Welfare and Family Law* 257–269

—— (2005) 'The Impact of the Marriage Act 1753: was it really "a most cruel law for the fair sex"?' 38(2) *Eighteenth Century Studies* 247–262

Probert, R and Barlow, A (2000) 'Displacing Marriage – Diversification and Harmonisation within Europe' 12(2) *Child and Family Law Quarterly* 153–165

Rake, K (ed) (2000) *Women's Incomes over the Lifetime* (London: The Stationery Office)

Rowthorne, R (2001) 'Marriage as a Signal' in A Dnes and R Rowthorn (eds), *The Law and Economics of Marriage and Divorce* (Cambridge, Cambridge University Press)

Sayer, RA (1992) (2nd ed) *Method in Social Science: a Realist Approach* (London, Routledge)

Schoen and Weinick (1993) 'Partner Choice in Marriage and Cohabitations' 55 *Journal of Marriage and Family* (May) 408–414

Scott, J, Braun, M and Alwin, D (1998) 'Partner, Parent, Worker: Family and Gender Roles', in R Jowell, J Curtice, A Park, L Brook, K Thomson and C Bryson (eds), *British and European Social Attitudes: the 15th Report – How Britain differs* (Aldershot, Ashgate)

Scottish Executive (2000) *Parents and Children* (Edinburgh, Scottish Executive)

Shaw, C and Haskey, J (1999) 'New Estimates and Projections of the Population Cohabiting in England and Wales' 95 *Population Trends* 7–17

Smart, C (2004) 'Changing Landscapes of Family Life: Rethinking Divorce' 3(4) *Social Policy and Society* 401–408

Smart, C and Stevens, P (2000) *Cohabitation Breakdown* (London and York, Family Policy Studies Centre/Joseph Rowntree Foundation)

Solicitors Family Law Association (2003) *Fairness for Families* (Orpington, SFLA)

Stone, L (1990) *Road to Divorce in England* (Oxford, Oxford University Press)

Sullivan, O (2000) 'The Division of Domestic Labour: twenty years of change?' 34(3) *Sociology* 437–456

Teubner, G (1993) 'Substantive and Reflexive Elements in Modern Law' 17(2) *Law and Society Review* 239–285

Théry, I, *Le Démariage* (Paris, Editions Odile Jacob)

Thornes, B and Collard, J (1979) *Who Divorces* (London, Routledge)

Waite, L and Gallagher, M (2000) *The Case for Marriage: Why Married People Are Happier, Healthier and Better Off Financially* (New York, Doubleday)

Ytterberg, H (2001) 'A Swedish Story of Love and Legislation' in R Wintermute and M Andenaes (eds), *Legal Recognition of Same-Sex Partnerships* (Oxford, Hart)

Index